Mumpreneur on Fire

4

MUMS IN BUSINESS ASSOCIATION

Edited and typeset by Fuzzy Flamingo
www.fuzzyflamingo.co.uk

To Jed & Obi,
I hope that Mummy can show you that anything is possible if you work hard enough. Everything I do is for you. Love you both with all my heart x

To Carter (my little genius), Freya (my little Diva) and Theo (my crazy afroman), Auntie loves you lots… now you're famous!

To my five beautiful children, you are my driving force. You mean more than you'll ever know. Love you to the moon and back xxx

Frazer, our honorary MIB, thank you for all of your continued support. Keep shining your light.

Acknowledgements

What a journey it has been. Here we are with the final book in the series, *Mumpreneur on Fire 4*.

Since launching the *Mumpreneur on Fire* series in 2017, Mums in Business Association has grown to over 37k followers on social media. We have helped to create over sixty-five best-selling authors so far and cannot wait to see what the future will bring.

Massive shout out to every single of one our tribe who support us, share our success and kick our arse when we need it!

For anyone out there who is feeling like they have had enough and can't take anymore… know that you are strong… you are amazing and you are capable of anything you set you mind to… just like the twenty-five incredible authors who have shared their journeys in this book!

Be inspired and never give up!

Introduction

Since launching Mums in Business Association in June 2017, sisters and co-founders Estelle Keeber and Leona Burton have been able to connect and inspire 37,000 social media followers in eighteen months!

Mums in Business Association is now proud to announce networking events ALL over the world, including Barbados and Australia. MIBA have great support from the BBC and have been mentioned in *The Sun*, *Best* magazine, *Thrive Global* as well as many more amazing publications.

Alongside all of the media coverage and success, both co-founders have also been nominated for awards in 2018!

Going forward, Estelle and Leona hope to continue to support and inspire thousands more women all over the world.

Mumpreneur on Fire 4 tells the stories of twenty-five more incredible women who, against all odds, have become inspiring mumpreneurs.

To find out more about Mums in Business Association check out the website: www.mumsinbusinessassociation.com

Contents

1. Karin

I wasn't one of those kids that knew what they wanted to do when they grew up… I mean, one week it was a nurse, the next a fighter pilot and somewhere along the line I wanted to be Simon Le Bon's wife. I was an RAF brat; my dad was posted every three years and my brother and I were taken along for the ride. I am not going to waffle on about my childhood here, I'm pretty sure a shrink would have a wild theory of why I destroyed seven Barbies with purple nail varnish and Tippex, but all in all I had your pretty average childhood with several hundred pets.

I moved to Scotland at sixteen years old, having just left school. I was slightly disappointed that all men didn't wear kilts, but when I realised the sun only came out six days a year I totally got why trousers are more practical. I settled into college and met a boy. He was Scottish. I couldn't actually understand what he was saying half the time, so I nodded and smiled a lot in the beginning. We got engaged and a few months after I found a bun in the oven. We ended up married in our teens with a child on the way. I lost count of the number of people who said we were stupid…

Well Mr and Mrs Stupid had our first born a few months later.

Life took over after that, I worked a succession of part-time jobs, our son Cameron being born two years after Kerry. A few years later, one night our TV stopped working and I fell pregnant with my third child, Georgia. I had been working part-time for several months when I announced my pregnancy. The boss was none too pleased. When I had a threatened miscarriage at ten weeks, I was signed off work for two weeks. I went back after one week to find I had been sacked. His reason? "You can't guarantee this won't happen again and I can't be doing with unreliable staff." He actually thought he could sack me because I was pregnant! HELL NO!

I went to a tribunal. My five minutes of fame followed shortly after I won an award at the tribunal and I appeared in a full page spread of the *Daily Mail* with the headline: "Hardworking mother of two sacked for pregnancy", with a photo of me looking like an overweight walrus standing wistfully looking out of the window.

More part-time jobs followed, and a house bought. In this time, I decided that I wanted to join the police. It was something I had always had an interest in, but I thought that I didn't stand a chance of getting in – I mean a mum of thirty with three young kids – but it turns out they didn't mind the old woman that lived in a shoe!

I joined up in 2002. I actually had a career.

My job was great; stressful but a challenge and fulfilling for the most part. In the meantime, my marriage was over. It broke my heart when I made the decision to end it. We both agreed the kids were first before anything else. I was working shifts, so it made sense that the kids stayed where they were, and I moved out. I moved in to my friend's spare bedroom and tried to convince myself I was doing the right thing.

It turned out we both did the right thing. We have three amazing kids who are well adjusted, not overly scarred by our break up, nor our transition to new partners – well it has not resulted in counselling for any of them and we have had no reported incidents of attempted murder in the family, so all's well that ends well. We are both very proud of our kids. Slightly concerned that my son does say he won't be forking out for my funeral and I will be chucked in a skip... so, in the event you are reading this Cameron... I am leaving you my collection of *Duran Duran* posters and my solar-powered headband torch... and you will never find where I buried the money!

Life skipped a few years after our divorce. My parents divorced, I bought their house and they moved on with their lives. I haven't seen my mother and brother in fourteen years now. I worked and I slept and had a radio on 24/7 to fill the silence in my empty house. My love life? A couple of long-term dalliances then a five week fling.

2

A few weeks after I ended it, I suddenly became ill. I couldn't keep anything down, I vomited after eating anything and gagged when I didn't eat. The weight started to fall off me. A stone in two weeks with no sign of feeling better, I grudgingly went to the docs. The first thing she asked: "Could you be pregnant?" Test says no. A week later I'm lying on a bed whilst being scanned and the nurse asks me to get dressed and return to the waiting room until she gets a doctor in. She wouldn't tell me what she saw on the screen – she turned it away from me. Tears streaming down my face, I returned to the waiting room and waited to be told I was dying. Yes, I had seen *Take a Break* magazine and knew how these stories worked… there was a huge growth, it would be inoperable and the doc was coming to tell me to write a will (I did mention my overactive imagination, didn't I?). I was called back in, the scan resumed.

Murmuring, pointing at the screen and I closed my eyes as I waited for the words, "I'm sorry to tell you…" Instead, he said, "Twins." I looked around… no TV cameras. No Jeremy Beadle… not an episode of *Punked*… TWINS!

Men that wear cagoules are not to be trusted. They don't tell you when the cagoule lets in the rain so you can go and get a brolly. They just don't say a word and hope you don't get wet. You follow me? Anyway, suffice to say he didn't want to know about babies and I didn't object.

I developed a taste for living in leggings, eating olives and crunching ice. My twin terrorists were born five weeks early. Cagoule boy wasn't fussed and, apart from asking their names and weights, I never heard from him again.

I took the boys home three weeks later and went back to work part-time when they were three months old. The boys went to an amazing childminder costing more than half of my wages, whilst I desperately tried to prove that I was just as good at my job and capable as a part-timer.

There were several times I thought about giving up my career in those early months. My shift got changed with three weeks' notice for a three-day event and I couldn't get anyone to take four-month-old twins from 7pm to 7am. I begged for a swap to a day shift and explained why… I got threatened with discipline if I didn't do the duty. I considered leaving the twins at home in their cots. Yes, I did. I am still angry that I felt so backed into a corner that I would even contemplate that. Welfare said I had a good legal case and to fight. In the end, my dad drove over from Ireland and arrived half an hour before I had to leave for my three night shifts.

When the boys were a few months old I met a man who I went on to spend three and a half years living with. I am happy to say I had a lucky escape. He was very good at hiding his true self in front of anyone but me… he was exposed when I recorded him one night. It got worse now he no longer had to hide his true nature. I finally discovered my kahunas after he had kept me up one night, interrogating me, making fake phone calls to intimidate me and I had to block the bedroom door with a chest of drawers, hugging my crying babies. Enough was enough… when he left for work in the morning, I took the boys to the childminder, went into work and this time the bosses came up top trumps and within an hour of revealing what I was going through, they had consulted the force lawyer and got the domestic abuse unit out with an alarm in my house. I regret to this day that I didn't officially report this man for what he did, but I knew it was mostly my word against his and, in the end, I opted for getting him out of my life. It took some time, as he continued to let me know he was outside watching for some weeks after that.

Months passed and, on the day I decided that men were only really good for getting rid of spiders, I met Paul. We got talking. We met within the week for a coffee and we talked for hours and hours. We were an item almost straight away.

A couple of months later, a friend messaged me with a screenshot of the front page of a national newspaper. There was my ex in handcuffs being led from the court. Abduction of a nurse it said. Sentenced to years in the clink at her majesty's pleasure.

The weeks that followed I cried a lot. Double-page spreads told the story of the nightmare that woman went through. I felt guilt. Guilt that I didn't do anything to prevent what that woman went through. I actually met the lady – we talked for hours and we had too much in common. One thing was clear, we were not to blame for his actions. That was all on him.

It took a lot for me to forgive myself after that meeting, but I moved house, changed my number and started again.

So back to happier days. Paul and I got engaged three months after we met and we moved in together with his daughter, who was eleven at the time. We got hitched in 2014 with not a cloud in the sky. We had an unfortunate incident of a randy cow and a guest's car, but that's for my next book.

2014 was an annus horribilis (as the queen might say). Everything that could go wrong, did go wrong. Paul and I decided to try for a baby because having to buy a people carrier was not enough... we wanted a minibus!! I had several early miscarriages and I was beginning to think my ovaries had shrivelled like raisins and it was never going to happen. Then when I really thought we were going to make the three-month mark, I started bleeding. I was at home on my days off. I hadn't told anyone I was pregnant, so went into work as normal on my next set of shifts.

Two of us on duty that night. I was standing in the middle of the street when blood started pouring out of me. I felt it gush and run down my legs into the top of my boots in seconds. I hastily told my colleague and radioed my supervisor. There was no one else on duty to take my place, so I drove home in the panda car, jumped in the shower, got changed and put a folded over tea towel in my granny pants just in case! Can you believe that I actually sat on a Tesco carrier bag in the panda (as I had bled out all over the driver's seat) and I drove back to work to finish my shift. At the end of the shift I had to phone the garage myself to pick up the panda to be cleaned. That was the most embarrassing and awful day ever.

I'm not sure where I lost my mojo, but after many hours of counselling, I suspect it was a culmination of all the things above and work. I had a supervisor who I felt made it his mission to make my life difficult, and somewhere along the line of budget cuts and understaffing, I started to get scared. Yes, scared. I began to worry about my safety. I began to dread going into work. When you are the only cop on duty for miles some days, the reality of being in situations where you might get hurt starts to play on your mind. I became a moaner – I ranted about the injustice, the cuts, the situations we were put in, the emphasis on targets, ticking boxes instead of people. This wasn't what I signed up to! I was beginning to dislike myself – I became everything I had avoided in others. I was so negative.

It was around mid-2015 that I decided to join a network marketing company in my spare time. Problems with my supervisor grew. I asked for a move, it was granted, then refused a week later. I won't go into the whole story because, if you heard it, you would probably be tempted to send him one of those packed full of glitter cards, so it takes him a week to hoover it out of his carpet and he still finds it in his pants four months later.

Looking back, I should have seen the signs. I was barely sleeping. I was coming in and sometimes getting two hours' sleep between shifts. I was exhausted and run down. I remember one time in the last two weeks I worked being suddenly aware that I was the only cop in the area for twenty miles. I didn't have a vehicle and I phoned my husband in tears as I walked back to the station at 4am in the morning. I believe that was my very first anxiety attack.

A couple of weeks went by, I was miserable and exhausted. Then halfway through my shift a call came in. As a cop, dead people are something you have to deal with. It's not nice, it may make you vomit, it may make you emotional, but at some point, you become used to it and see it as just another part of your job. What I saw that day will stay with me forever. The person had died the day before whilst having a bath. I tried to ignore floating organs and intestines on top of the water as I turned the tap off and tried to pull the plug. I went home that night and cried for an hour. That night I had a nightmare. The next night I fell into the same nightmare three times after waking up. The next night I drank coffee and slept little. The next night I didn't go to bed.

I was falling apart. I can't quite remember if it was the next set of shifts that it came to a head, but I remember it was the first day shift. I opened my emails to be told that my shifts were to be changed (when I had made plans). The next email was to say that I would not be excused court duty on my annual leave. The first time I had booked to travel to Ireland to see my dad in two years.

I lost it. Completely. Meltdown central…

Taxi for karin!

I went outside to have a ciggie and I started to shake. Uncontrollably. Then I started to sob. Tears were running down my face faster than I could catch them, and I was bent over double just sobbing and howling like an animal. Snotters hanging from my nose, mascara smeared down my cheeks, I had no idea where this had come from – I just knew I couldn't go back inside. I radioed the on-duty sergeant and I don't even know how she understood me, as my voice was so high I doubt even dogs could have heard me. I don't even remember what I said to her, but I remember saying I was leaving.

That day marked the start of a terrifying journey with anxiety. I rarely left the house for over nine months except for doctors' appointments and counselling. I stopped answering the phone, I never answered the door and I cancelled everything and everyone except my husband and kids. I didn't get dressed for approximately seven months. I was a mess. I had to be reminded to shower, and I could put a ponytail in my armpit hair. I resembled a yeti on weed most of the time and I had panic attacks daily. I couldn't breathe, I would sob and gulp and feel like my heart was going to explode out of my chest. I was startled at a cup being put down too hard. I couldn't deal with noise. I shook constantly, stopped paying bills, I ignored friends, made excuses rather than admit I was very ill, I left letters unopened and I stayed for hours at a time in my bedroom with frequent nightmares or suffered insomnia for days. My bosses thought my "episode" at work was an über-reaction. Seems I wasn't under any more stress than the rest of the cops out there and, when I returned, I would be going back to the same supervisor.

Many weekly counselling sessions followed, and the conclusion was that no I wasn't batshit crazy… my job was making me ill. I was called in to discuss a return to work, I went to the meeting, but had already decided my health had to come first. I expected more of the talking and not listening but this time new people were in the room… all change – we will move you – we will ease you back into work, you won't have to see your old supervisor. All smiles. Confused Karin.

At the end of the meeting, more bosses came in… I was told I was being investigated (one of my work from home team was a cop who held a planned party two hours after I was told to cease any affiliation with a home business), with a view to disciplinary proceedings as I had mentored her and profited, wait for it… a whole £11.87 from said party. It all became crystal clear… it made my decision easier. I resigned that day. My career was over. My letter spelled out exactly how I felt about my treatment and I felt I had to leave – the first step to my recovery.

A few weeks later, the realisation that I never had to go back. Relief transcended, and I began to slowly start to take care of me (who knew that shaved legs got so cold!), I started to wean myself off my medication. I started to leave the house, once every few weeks at first. I was still having full-blown anxiety attacks, but not nearly as often.

Resigning was the turning point, but I needed a job. I decided to go back to network marketing – it was the only option for me. In the house in Forever Friends PJs… I went like a rocket, made it my focus and quickly built my online presence as a network marketer… then the company folded.

I made a decision to go solo – I had £50 and that's what I started with. I started to advertise bath bombs I bought wholesale. A few weeks later, a friend asked me if she could sell them too… then another friend. Beauty Bath Junkie was born!

In April 2018, we moved into manufacturing premises, registered with the VAT man and I get dressed every day! I make my own products now, have many cosmetic safety assessments under my belt, and after registering with the VAT man I finally realised I have a successful business. As far as the future – who knows? It's true what all the gurus say… never make money your goal, make passion the thing that drives you… the money will follow (until the VAT man takes a chunk and that sucks big time, let me tell you).

In the meantime, I am open to offers from Richard Branson to buy me out and keep me on with a suitably high salary, company car, private healthcare plan and yearly trips to Necker Island. I'm thinking perhaps as creative director.

My goals:
• To be sold in Harrods. (Not me… just my bath bombs.)

- To have a tidy house.
- To have a holiday that lasts more than three days.
- To finish a cup of coffee before forgetting where I put it.
- To write a book where I tell you all about the saucy cow.

Over and out.

★ ★ ★

Karin lives in Fife, Scotland, with her husband Paul, two children and two fur babies. The rest of her brood are close by and you can usually find her in her workshop, caked in dye and glitter. When she's not working, she can be found spending time with her family, her dogs and her new grandbaba, with the occasional trip outside in the real world.

She would like to thank all the twatwaffles in her life who made her journey difficult, the ones who abandoned her, belittled her, bullied her, took advantage of her and thought she would never amount to much. If it wasn't for them, she wouldn't be where she is today.

She would also like to thank those who believed in her and supported her on her journey. She is especially eternally grateful to her husband Paul for his love, his late nights helping pack boxes and his coffee-making skills. If it wasn't for him, she would still be sitting in a corner rocking, eating her body weight in chocolate and crying when the milk ran out. A special mention to her twin terrorists Connor and McKenzie, who are a dab hand at shrink wrapping, labelling and painting bath bombs.

Karin is on Facebook and Instagram – Beauty Bath Junkie. If you ever have a passion for unicorns, mermaids, glitter, bath art and all things pamper, you can order at www.beautybathjunkie.co.uk

2. Michele L

This may shock some people, but from a very early age I had this intuition that I would never have a child of my own. I cannot explain why I felt this way, I just knew deep down inside that this was not something that would happen for me.

I remember when I was young that all my friends had dolls and pushchairs, but that never appealed to me, not one bit. I know that I am a maternal, kind and caring person, but being a mother and giving birth in all honesty terrified me. So, you can imagine the fear I had when I found out I was pregnant when I was nineteen years old; I was shitting myself, I will not lie. I was nineteen, and the boy who I thought I was going to be with forever had just split with me and wanted nothing to do with a baby; he had made that very, very clear. The only thing that made me excited was that my little sister was pregnant too, finally something we could share together. My baby, unfortunately, never made it into the world, but my sister's did, my beautiful and talented niece Summer, who has recently turned fourteen years old.

When my sister gave birth to Summer I cried so much, not only because I was happy, but also because I was heartbroken, as it should have been me. I know that may come across as selfish, but I was so hurt and grieving that all I could do was cry. I love my niece, she is, to my sister's annoyance, exactly like me in her mannerisms, artistic flare and attitude. Still, to this day, every time it is her birthday, or I see her, I think about that little baby that wasn't meant to be.

In December 2010, I went on a date that would change my life forever. We had been talking online for a few months after being introduced to one another by a mutual friend. Danny was recently divorced, a father of

10

two, seven years older than me and living in Northumberland, whereas I lived in Norfolk. I remember saying to our friend, "Why are you setting me up with him, how on earth do you think that will work?" I guess this friend knew more than we gave him credit for. On the 15th December 2010 Danny picked me up and we went to a beautiful country pub for our first date. This date was it for me, that day I fell in love with him and knew that was it. It was like one of those moments you love to watch on *First Dates* when the restaurant empties but you two are so caught up in each other you have no clue until the manager tells you he wants to go home.

Despite the distance, we managed to work it all out: he would come to see me for weekends, I would get a train on a Friday after work to go see him and travel back late on a Sunday night. In the February of 2011, Danny proposed and we made plans to move in with each other and get married in December 2012 on the anniversary of our first date. Our bubble was about to pop; we found out that Danny was due to be deployed to the Falklands for four months. I could not imagine four months of not seeing him; even when thinking about it now I cry. He is my best friend, so whenever I have to say goodbye to him it breaks me; any military wife will understand exactly what I mean.

The summer of 2012 was the first time I met Danny's children. I was so nervous, as anyone would be, as you just want them to like you to make things run smoothly. We were going on holiday with them and Danny's parents to a wooden cabin in a forest on the Norfolk coast. I have to say, on this trip things went quite well, but it was clear that the children were maybe not keen or annoyed their dad had a girlfriend. I can't identify exactly what it was, but a flag went up. We made the most of the holiday and then it was back to me and Danny being alone before he flew out in October ready to return in January 2013. While Danny was away, we found out he would be posted to work permanently in Norfolk, so I found us a house to rent ready to start our life together. Danny and I both found this time apart really hard and, as a result, when he came back we split up. This was only for a short period and we had remained in contact through the short break; we joke now that it was like Ross and Rachel in *Friends* ("We were on a break"). All joking aside, I was heartbroken, and now worrying that I was going to have to pay for this house by myself and cancel all the wedding stuff. Danny was great and cancelled all that, so I didn't have to. He also moved in the first night he moved to Norfolk. I remember I was sitting at work and he texted to ask what I was doing for dinner. He suggested coming over for dinner and a talk, asking if he could move in, so we started our life together again. We decided that we would get married in the October 2013, which we did. It was a very small ceremony with myself and my best friend, his best man and E and K, Danny's children. It was a lovely short ceremony and then we had a party with all our family and friends on the Friday.

We moved into military housing and this was the start of my entrepreneurial journey. I had just left a pretty decent job in insurance, but I hated it. I left a few months before we got married due to illness through stress, so I reassessed my passions and trained as a massage and beauty therapist. So, once we moved, I set up my new business and started to do mobile appointments as well as appointments from home. In this time, we also discussed having children. As Danny had two and I had none, we started to look at options as to how we could have a child of our own as Danny had unfortunately had a vasectomy before we even met. We went to a doctor and were told we would be looking at around £20,000 to medically make it happen for us to have a biological child. Now I know I said I never wanted children, but when I fell in love, and I mean real love with Danny, I wanted his children. Every time I saw him with his children and how much of a great dad he was I wanted his children; I still do every time I see him interact with them, or how he is with a friend's child, something inside me breaks. It is a pain that I can't describe, but I am sure there are hundreds of women who know what I am talking about.

Anyway, after the shock of being told how much it would be, we looked at the process of adoption and we decided to go down this route. We knew that we could love a child that wasn't biologically ours as I love his children, so the biological side of things mattered less. We made our application, met our adoption social worker, went on a course where we met some other amazing people who were on their own journey to becoming a family and then got to the end of stage one. The next stage would have been us going down the route to panel and then finding our child, or children. This was about a year after we had been married. Then one morning Danny had a call that would change us and our lives forever. E was coming to live with us full time! I was about to go from looking for our child to becoming a mother figure overnight to a child who at the time I was still convinced did not actually like me. I was terrified and, I will not lie, pretty pissed off. I even thought that it was done on purpose, like maybe I was just not meant to have my happy ending.

E moved in the next day. I managed to get him into the local school straight away so that he was not missing out on education and I had managed to get his own room all sorted so he had a space to call his own, as he really needed it. He came to live with us as a very angry, hurt and emotional young boy. He was only nine when this happened and, although he loves his dad and wanted to always live with him, he missed his brother and sister and home life with his mum. I think at nine he just really couldn't process what was happening, so this manifested as rage, a lot of rage! Now I had not spent any time alone with him before, and the most time we had all been together was two weeks, and now I was the one who was spending all the time with him and the person he was taking all his emotions out on. I cried pretty much every day for a year because I was annoyed, I was angry, I was frustrated and I was feeling so upset for this little boy who could not control what he was feeling or say how he was feeling; at nine you don't know the words for things like this. I work with adults who struggle to find words for how they feel. It was demanding on both myself and my husband and, as a result, my beauty business stopped so I could concentrate on helping E, plus I was suffering with my own mental health due to what was going on.

I worked very hard with the school who managed to get a counsellor to help E when he was having a bad day, to help the teachers work with him and his behaviour. I also worked with the doctors to get him into play therapy to help him deal with his emotions, which was starting to work and we started to get some kind of family routine going. E still had good and bad days, but the good days were becoming more frequent than the bad; we were all starting to get on and enjoy life. Then I lost my grandfather at a period where E was starting to play up again. He had just gone into high school where he was no longer getting the support of a counsellor and had a teenage attitude, as well as his emotions now being in full swing with a nice dose of hormones.

My grandfather was someone I massively looked up to and someone who I just thought would always be around. He was the healthiest, most active person in their late eighties I had ever seen. His death came as a massive shock. I went to bed knowing he was in hospital and going to have tests the next day. I remember being asleep and something or someone said, "Michele". I woke up and could see my phone flashing. I had loads of missed calls from my mum, my sister and my sister's boyfriend. I called my mum and she said, "Grandad's gone." I just broke down and sobbed my heart out. This was the first time I had lost anyone that important to me. I was really close to him and now I would never see him again. His death sent me into a spiral of mental health problems; I just couldn't cope with that and E. I went to my doctor and asked for help; I pretty much begged. His answer: "I can give you some tablets to numb it, so you can get through the funeral." I do not understand why that is the answer to someone who is desperate for help; this is where I decided, "Fuck it, I will help myself!"

I delved heavily into self-help books, personal development, I followed motivational women, listened to podcasts, absorbing as much as I could and, although the emotional pain was still not great, I managed to find ways to cope. I even started a life coaching diploma to help others who were in similar positions as myself; it also gave me a lot of tools to help myself and E with his issues. I passed my diploma and hired a business coach. I was all ready to go and start my new business as a life coach when shit started to hit the fan with E again; he was really struggling with school and the whole school environment, as a result taking it out on people at school, students and teachers, as well as causing issues at home. So, my husband and I spoke to the school, I even went in to have a meeting with them to explain his story and how they could help him. They promised me the earth and then the following day he went into school and was confronted by ten children who wanted to kick the shit out of him and threatened him. Some of these children where in year eleven (sixteen-year-olds); he was in year eight. We spoke to the school and did our own investigating as to what we could do. I spoke to a lady I knew who homeschooled and mentioned it to Danny. We investigated it further, the outside help we could get, and spoke to E to see what he wanted and how he was feeling. We all decided that as the school could not keep him safe, and the other schools in the area were either worse or had long waiting lists, I would homeschool him. I did so for six months and it was one of the hardest things I have ever had to do.

E never really listens to me anyway and had a few issues with women and authority, so this was a big challenge, as well as managing his mental health and behavioural issues. It got to a stage when he totally lost it with me and, as a result, I had to lock myself in my kitchen. E was now thirteen and 5ft 8, I am only 5ft 4, so yes, he was now intimidating. I almost left my husband twice in this period, which breaks my heart to say as I love him so much. I do also love E, but it was so much pressure on me; I felt so bloody helpless as I was trying everything I could to help and it was thrown back in my face over and over again. It was demoralising!

I have arranged so much counselling and assessments for E to get him help, but the waiting list for things like this is so long and ridiculous that once you go down one avenue recommended by a doctor, you spend six months waiting to then be told that service is not right for him, so they say to go back to a doctor and get another referral. We are still waiting now to get some help for him. He just finds dealing with emotions so hard and gets very angry. It is sad as he is such a great boy and, despite everything, we do have a good relationship, he does confide in me, and we have a good laugh as a family. There are bad days and good days, but now the good days really do outweigh the bad days.

I never say I am E's mum, I have told him that I don't want to be called Mum, as he has a mum and that is not me. I am his stepmum and will always treat him the way I would if he was my own son because that is the person I am and the love I have for him. He has lived with us for four years. These years that we have spent as a family have been bloody hard, but you know what, we are a bloody strong family because of it. I figure if we can go through all the upset, pain and emotions we had in that four-year period and survive, we can do anything.

It is also thanks to E that I have found my passion work-wise in life. I started my blog *She Steps Up* to deal with the mental health issues I was having and the effect that being a stepparent had on me. The reason it is called *She Steps Up* is because I am a stepmum who 'Stepped Up' when this little boy needed me. I then realised that there are so many more women in this world that step up daily and this is how my feature 'Women of Wisdom' was born. 'Women of Wisdom' is where I interview amazing empowering women all over the world who are kicking ass in business and life. This has allowed me to meet and speak to so many amazing inspiring women and got me noticed as a mentionable motivator and feature in the press with Tony Robbins.

Due to loving my blog so much and finding my passion of writing I have now combined that with my passion for sales and social media to set up my copywriting and coaching business as a social media and business strategist for female entrepreneurs; my life coaching diploma wasn't wasted either, thankfully. I know that if I had not gone down this crazy path and done the work I have with E and within myself I would not have been able to find this passion and start my business from home.

Thanks to this, I am now on a mission to build my business into a multiple six-figure business, to help thousands of women all over the world find their authentic voice, to stand out in a crowd and get seen by their dream clients and bring in their own six figures. I plan to do as much writing as I can and leave my footprint on the world, while inspiring and motivating other women to believe in themselves and go for what they deserve. My personal goals are that I want to be able to retire my husband from the military so that he no longer misses out on his children growing up and turning into young adults; I also want to make sure E has his dad here with him. I plan to make a life where we can see the world, exploring together and get E into a university, as he is a clever young man who has great plans of becoming an engineer. He has already excelled at computer programming at thirteen, so I know he will go far.

My message for you, whoever you are, is to know that no matter what life throws your way, expected or unexpected, know that it can be hard, really hard, but you are so much stronger than you think and you have it inside you to kick ass and take it all on, and create something magical from it all.

★ ★ ★

Michele Marie is a military wife and full-time stepmum who lives in Norfolk, UK. Michele Marie is a social media and business strategist helping female entrepreneurs find their authentic voice, stand out in a crowd and make the impact on the world they desire. Michele Marie is also focused on helping women get seen and inspire other women through her blog *She Steps Up*.

You can find Michele Marie at:
Blog – www.shestepsup.com

3. Laura H

Growing up I had a very normal life; it was my sister and I and our amazing parents. They worked hard to provide us with everything that we needed and to give us a good education. Education was really important. We were sent to the best private school in the area and, as children, we didn't know any different, but looking back at the experiences and exposure that we had there we were very, very lucky. I look back at my school days very fondly.

I left school and went to university. I wanted to be a journalist writing for a women's beauty magazine, so I was studying English Literature and, in my final year, I also decided to train in beauty therapy and as a make-up artist. I really enjoyed doing this and also had a part-time job in the beauty department of one of the large department stores.

As time progressed, I applied to go to journalism college and sent letter after letter to editors and deputy editors of women's magazines trying to get work experience placements. I was fortunate enough to gain a placement at a mass media company in London and off I went to the big smoke to see how everything was done.

I was so disappointed. In my youthful naivety I hadn't realised that products were not necessarily featured due to their merit but because they were sent to the magazines by PR companies gaining exposure for their clients. I had so much knowledge about active ingredients of products, skin types and product combinations, not to mention the make-up skills that I had acquired. I actually knew my stuff and no one else seemed to. It was incredibly disheartening. At this point I continued with my application for journalism college, but my heart wasn't in it. All that I had ever wanted to be was a journalist – I now knew that that wasn't what I wanted to do, but I didn't know what I did want to do.

I remember walking through the west end the day that my placement ended, incredibly downcast and a little bit lost. It was then that my phone rang. Earlier in the year I had applied for a job as cabin crew with an airline. I had wanted to make sure that my summer after university was interesting and exciting. I didn't want another summer of temping whilst I waited for college to start in September. I hadn't travelled much and wanted to see some new places, so this had seemed like a perfect way to do this. I hadn't thought any more about it until now and they were inviting me for an interview. It felt like the answer to my issues right then. In one phone call I had gone from not knowing what I wanted in the future to at least knowing pretty much what I would be doing over the summer.

I went for my assessment day and made it through each round until eventually I had my interview. At the end of the day, I was offered the position on the spot. To be honest, the whole day hadn't really felt like an assessment – it had been really fun, so it was a fantastic ending to an already great day.

I actually started my cabin crew training before I had finished my degree, but as I hadn't yet sat my final exams, I was given special leave to go back at exam time. So, by the time my university course had finished, I had already pretty much wrapped up and moved back home to complete my cabin crew training and to start flying.

So, life in the skies began; I absolutely loved it. Working each day with different crew and dealing with different issues. There is no doubt that it was hard work on our feet all day (and night), working odd days and hours and never really knowing what time of day or which day (!!) it was. The travel bug had hit me hard. My initial summer contract was due to finish at the end of October, so I started to make plans to travel for a couple of months during the winter months. I planned my route through Asia and Australia and off I went on my own.

I met some great friends travelling around and am still close now to some of them. It's very easy to be happy when you are travelling and experiencing new places, mostly being on the beach every day. We didn't have a care in the world. As Christmas was drawing near and the time for me to return to the UK was coming close, my friends in Oz were making their plans for Christmas. The DJ Judge Jules was playing on Bondi Beach on Christmas Day – I wanted in. I changed my flights and stayed on. Now that I am a mum, I feel so guilty; my poor mum loves Christmas, it is an important family time and I had just ditched everyone in favour of the beach. I know that my girls will do this to me one day and I suppose it is all a part of growing up and letting your children grow up and being happy for them.

Eventually, I flew back to the UK. I landed in the dreary grey cold and miserable weather at Heathrow. I loved seeing my family again, but life was a bit flat. I was waiting for the next summer season to start flying but I was driving my parents mad. I was living in their house and to coin a phrase used by parents of teenagers/young adults everywhere 'treating it like a hotel'. I think my parents had wondered why they had spent absolute fortunes on my education for me to be doing nothing. Their patience had run out with me and quite rightly so, they didn't need to be working hard bankrolling me. My mum sat me down with the job section of the local paper and made me start applying. With a heavy heart I told the airline that I wouldn't be coming back, and I started the applications. The problem was that I still didn't know what I wanted to do. I knew that journalism wasn't for me, but because I had been entirely focused on writing and journalism, I felt that I didn't have any relevant experience to do anything else and I still didn't know what to do. Nothing was lighting me up.

Not too much time passed, and I got a job as a trainee surveyor. I was also working part-time in a restaurant to pay my parents back the money they had lent to me. I was super busy but I was a bit lonely as I didn't really have any friends locally and so had to start again. It was then that I met one of my best ever friends. We worked together and at first sight we didn't really get each other. She thought I talked too slowly, I thought she was a bit crazy. However, as we got to know each other, we both understood each other; we were very similar, two very girlie girls and our adventures began. We had great fun together and got in some real scrapes. She honestly kept me sane in that time. I worked very hard in those days, nine-to-five in the office and six-to-midnight most evenings, and then at weekends as well. I wanted to show my parents that I had appreciated everything that they had done for me and pay them back.

I just didn't enjoy the dreary nine-to-five. I know that there are thousands of people who don't enjoy their jobs, but it is obviously having to work. I just couldn't reconcile in my head that for my working life I would be doing something so tedious. A surveyor I wasn't. So, I made a decision – I would either go back and study further again and do something with my beauty qualifications or I would go back to flying. Whilst I was investigating training courses and career options, I was also applying for flying jobs. I had itchy feet again, so it is perhaps not surprising to hear that I handed my notice in and flew off to the US. Las Vegas and Colorado were calling and after an amazing few weeks away I came back and pretty much walked straight into another flying job. Although I was back in the skies and once again loving life, I was working for another charter airline on a summer contract. I wanted a permanent position, so I was still applying to the scheduled airlines. Pretty soon an interview came up and I switched airlines.

This started a new chapter of my life. It was on my first proper trip away that I met my husband. It was the hugest cliché of all, the cabin crew and the pilot, but we didn't care. We had a lot of fun, he was so lovely (still is), so polite (actually quite rare) and he really took care of me. Which is why the bottom fell out of my world when approximately six months into our relationship he said that he wanted to go and live in Dubai. He had been offered a job out there and wanted to go. As far as I was concerned it probably wasn't going to work between us – I had done long distance relationships before and they didn't work. I didn't see how this could be any different. I would need a visa to live in Dubai as, under the conservative Islamic local law, it is illegal for unmarried couples to live together. I said that I wouldn't go out there without a job to support myself.

I helped him pack up his belongings and drove him off to Heathrow to fly off to his new life. I was gutted – it felt so unfair. I kept thinking, 'Why is this happening again to me, why can't I be happy?' I started to apply for jobs and flew out to visit him when I had a run of days off in my flying schedule. The first time I made it out to visit was actually the first anniversary of when we met. It was amazing to see each other, but he was behaving very oddly, and I was getting very irritated with him; little did I know that he was planning to propose and his behaviour was all because he was petrified.

Fast forward a little over a year and we were happily married with a baby. Living the Dubai dream. I absolutely loved having my little girl and Dubai is an amazing place. I went to mum and baby groups so that my little one could meet some friends and in time I also made some friends (still some of my best friends now). Our network expanded and over time so did our family. There were now five of us. We are absolutely blessed to have had three little girls.

Unfortunately, it was just after the birth of my third daughter that my health deteriorated. I woke up one day with excruciating pain in my neck and also in my feet. I couldn't move my neck or walk properly. I was in agony. A trip to the doctors and some blood tests later showed a diagnosis of Rheumatoid Arthritis – this autoimmune disorder can flare up after pregnancy. Thankfully my case was not too severe, and we managed to get my symptoms under control.

At around the same time I was putting off going for a smear test – my ob-gyn had told me to book in following my pregnancy, but I kept putting it off. Earlier in the year, I had started working again and it was hard to fit everything in – running the girls around to school and nursery and activities and working. So, it was probably ten months before I went and finally booked the appointment. When the doctor called and said that I had to go back for further tests I wasn't too worried. However, I was told that I needed to have surgery to remove part of my cervix as the cells were showing early stage cancer cells. As the cancerous cells hadn't yet invaded other cells the doctor would be able to remove them, which she did. Unfortunately I had to have follow up surgery as I suffered from some complications after the procedure. This made the whole process incredibly long and drawn out. However, I was lucky. A smear test is something that I will never ever put off again. Five minutes of discomfort in the doctor's office can make all the difference.

Following the surgery, I was feeling very down, I was piling on the pounds and wallowing in my misery. I couldn't go to the beach or go swimming and I felt disgusting. This was when everything spiralled. I loved my job and remember working from my hospital bed still groggy from anaesthetic. I loved my family and enjoyed running the girls around and enjoying life with my husband. I was running myself into the ground trying to be all things to everyone. It was not sustainable.

My joints started aching and flaring up again, I was suffering with stomach ache and digestive issues, my skin was covered in a rash and I was absolutely exhausted. My attitude became very negative, the glass was definitely half empty. My inner voice was negative and, looking back now, anxiety had started to creep in.

I remember one Saturday morning taking my eldest to a netball practice and sitting on the floor to watch her; it was completely beyond me to talk to any of the other parents. My body was hurting all over and all that I wanted to do was sleep. I cried as I watched her that day. I saw the other parents coming and going and couldn't understand why I felt so different to them. Yes, I had three children and was busy running them around, yes my husband travelled so wasn't always there to help out, but we had a full-time nanny who lived with us and helped with the children and the house and I wasn't doing anything that other parents weren't. Why couldn't I function? I tried to go to the gym and exercise classes, but it was a real effort putting one foot in front of the other; it was as if I had lead weights in my shoes. All of this added to my own sense of failure and negativity.

I decided that enough was enough. I was fed up of stumbling around like a zombie and something had to change. I took myself back to the doctors. The doctor ordered so many blood tests that the nurse had to double check that he hadn't selected all of them in error. I was diagnosed this time with Fibromyalgia, which is widespread pain throughout the body from an undetermined cause, and Lyme Disease – an infectious disease which is spread by ticks. As the Lyme Disease was being investigated with further tests, the doctor started to treat the fibromyalgia and I started taking medication. I started to feel a lot better and had slightly more energy. Little by little, life was improving.

My dad turned seventy that summer and we had hired a villa in Sri Lanka for the whole family to enjoy together. I flew from Dubai to Colombo with my parents and, on the flight, I realised that I had left all of my medication at home. We tried to work out whether someone could send it to us, but by the time it would get to me our holiday would be almost finished. I would just have to go cold turkey and stop taking the meds. I knew that the doctor had advised against this, she had said that I would need to come off them gradually, but we had been planning to do this upon my return anyway. I felt horrendous, I kept having what felt like brain zaps, I had a fever and terrible headaches. I decided that if this is what happened when I stopped taking the medication, I really didn't want to be taking it anyway, so I continued the withdrawal and told the doctor what had happened when I returned to Dubai. By the time I saw her the drugs were out of my system anyway, I was no longer suffering from withdrawal effects and my energy was back up again.

Life is very busy with children, especially in Dubai. There are a lot of early starts for sports practices as it is mostly too hot in the afternoon after school. So, most mornings at 6.30am the children of Dubai are swimming lengths of the pool, running around a track or fitting in an extra music practise all before school starts at 7.30am. My girls are involved in everything, so it wasn't long before I was running myself into the ground again. Getting up before 5am each day, leaving the house at 6am going to sports practices, then school and nursery runs, then work before doing it all over again in the afternoon. More school and nursery runs and then afterschool activities. I was fading again. I was a wreck physically and emotionally.

My stomach issues were also becoming unbearable. I couldn't function in day-to-day life I was in so much pain. I was admitted to hospital again and the gastro doctor performed an endoscopy to have a look at my stomach. There was so much acid in my stomach that he had to remove it. He described the lining of my stomach as showing scratches and these scratches were ulcerated. We were due to fly to France the following week for a skiing holiday, so I was really keen to not hang around in the hospital. The doctor agreed to discharge me and allow me to travel if I followed the medication schedule and came back to see him when I returned. I jumped at the chance, so off we went to France with a suitcase rattling full of medication. My health improved whilst we were away – nothing like fresh mountain air and getting away from hectic life to make you feel better. When I went back to see the doctor, he asked me if I was stressed.

I said that I didn't have anything to be stressed about – I couldn't see that stress was clearly playing a huge part in my life.

When we returned from France, I also made an appointment to see a specialist rheumatologist. I knew that I needed to get to the bottom of my health issues and I wanted my life back. She suggested that I go to see a physio for a specialised technique called NST – there is only one licensed practitioner for this technique in Dubai, so I made an appointment. NST is a technique where the practitioner applies pressure to specific muscles in your body whilst directing you to breathe deeply. This resets the natural vibrations within your body. It was all a bit kooky for me, but there was a science behind it and, as I said, I was at breaking point, I would try anything. With this mentality in mind, I also changed the way I was eating and started following a GAPS diet to heal my digestive system. The doctor had said to me that the stomach is our second brain. Our brain cannot function properly if our stomach isn't functioning properly, the two are intrinsically connected. She also told me that I needed to work on my breathing as I wasn't breathing properly.

At the same time, I decided that I was going to have reiki. A friend had recommended it to me previously, but it wasn't something that I knew anything about and again thought it was a bit kooky, a bit out there. Out of the blue, a friend sent me the details for a reiki practitioner. I am a great believer in being in the right place at the right time and things happening at the right time. The way of the universe. So, I gave it a go. This is when everything began to fall into place. The reiki practitioner was a lovely lady who instantly calmed and centred me. In my first couple of sessions she also told me that I didn't breathe properly and needed to work on my breathing. She also reiterated the doctor's sentiments that your gut health is paramount for all over wellbeing. I didn't need any more signs – I knew that I was on the right path to recovery.

I progressed through my reiki sessions and also did some coaching sessions. I learnt that I needed to put myself first without feeling guilty, to make time for myself and believe in myself. I could only be the best for my children if I led by example. Show them that you believe in yourself and they will believe in themselves. I really connected with myself and made small changes in my life. Small changes can make a big difference and, within a short time, I had completely turned everything around. My health improved dramatically, the stress that I hadn't been able to recognise before dissipated away and my energy was different. Not only my energy levels but the energy I was sending out to the world and therefore the energy that I was receiving back.

With my new positive outlook and renewed self-belief, I started my own business as a virtual assistant – something that I had previously talked myself out of. My business is growing daily, and I have huge plans for the future.

The message that I want people to take away from my story is go for it. Whatever it is in life that you want to do, go for it. Your self-belief and determination will see you through, no-one else really cares what other people are doing, so instead of being your own biggest critic be your own cheerleader. Be kind to yourself and find people that lift you up, never stop learning. Mums in Business Association was instrumental in my development and made me realise that everyone has wobbles, you just need to carry on regardless.

★ ★ ★

Laura is thirty-five and lives in Dubai with her husband and three daughters. She works as a virtual assistant supporting other small businesses. She also coaches and supports other virtual assistants to set up their own business. www.laurahilmi.com

4. Stacey M

If I'm totally honest, I can't remember much of my childhood and some of the things I thought happened didn't actually happen like I remember. I remember playing in the front garden with my sister as my dad packed up his car and left our family home when he and mum separated. I remember playing and laughing and rolling around on the grass with Shannan, but this never actually happened; he left while we were sleeping.

I do, however, remember picking up my GCSE results with my grandad just after I'd had my braces removed. He waited outside in the car, I opened my results envelope with him and he was so incredibly proud of me. He wasn't surprised, though, as I was always quite bright and academic, and everyone had high expectations of me. I was wise beyond my years and the one with her head screwed on, or so they thought.

Truth is, throughout my teen years I had no real idea who I was, and this made building close friendship bonds difficult. I had lots of friendship groups and got on with everyone, but never developed any long lasting connections.

I continuously tried to people please, to fit in and be noticed.

I didn't really know where I fit in the world and I felt invisible most of the time, so when my sister got poorly and my mum's time had to be devoted to supporting her in hospital and at home, I felt so alone and I grieved our closeness!

I'd lost my guide and, through yearning for that closeness elsewhere, I made some pretty crappy decisions, which had an impact on how I felt about myself and how I viewed relationships as a whole, but that's for another book.

Then I met Dan; he noticed me in the nightclub that night, he knew who I was. Mr popular who had this Jack the Lad, bad boy reputation recognised me; he knew the geeky, short girl with braces who always felt invisible.

Like most boys with his reputation, he tried to get me to go back to his that night; obviously I turned him down. He disappeared, so I was glad I hadn't made another crappy decision again, through wanting to feel close to someone.

Just as I was leaving, he returned, asking for my number and, over the next few weeks, he was persistent and never gave up wanting to meet up again. Even after my constant knock backs. He still wanted me, so I agreed. He picked me up and the whole date we spoke and laughed, and it felt so comfortable.

I could be completely myself and I didn't feel so alone and invisible when I was with him!

We really hit it off and, although he worked away, we constantly messaged each other. He would pick me up from work and we would either grab a movie from blockbuster and share a Thai chicken curry or be out drinking with friends. I still find it fascinating how he could find me attractive after holding my hair back while I spewed all the Corky's white chocolate alcohol shots back up.

Everything was great; Mum and Shan were home again and I was busy living life as a spontaneous, carefree eighteen-year-old.

Life was awesome, I was having fun and loved how Dan knew me better than I knew myself. We spoke about children and families and all of the grown-up stuff and in the new year it all happened quicker than we expected.

At eighteen years and three months, my period didn't show. I texted Dan and asked him to take me to get a test before our arranged cinema date that evening. He dropped me off at home; Mum was at work, so I decided to take the test. I remember taking the instruction leaflet out and reading and re-reading it again to make sure I peed on this stick correctly, thinking if I did it wrong, it would give me an inaccurate answer... like seriously, how hard is it to just pee on a stick, right?

So, I peed on the stick and sat there staring at the window on the test, heart pounding with that fearful sick feeling you get in the pit of your stomach.

The first line was instant then the second line appeared… my heart pounds remembering it. I was shaking, the adrenaline consumed me, I grabbed the leaflet and read it again, triple-checking what this cross on the test meant.

Did a cross mean it was negative, like when you get an answer wrong in your test and the teacher puts an x by it… holy shit balls… a cross meant positive. I got the second test out and was determined to pee again just to be sure… I sat there, hand between my knees, holding the second test in the trickle of wee, trying to make it last the whole five seconds… and wait again… one line… two lines… FUCK!

'I am!' I texted him. 'You are what? X' he replied… *what do ya think 'I am' means,* I thought to myself… 'PREGNANT', I messaged back. 'Do you still want to go to the cinema?' Seriously, who even thinks about going to the cinema just after they've found out they are pregnant, by someone they met three months ago, who has never met your parents, who has a reputation of being a Jack the Lad man-whore?

My priorities were obviously still a bit skewed at this point.

Meanwhile, Mum had noticed I'd not been myself during my missed period week and knew I hadn't yet come on, so had been texting me all day checking in on me and implied that it may be a good idea to do a test to make sure. I hesitantly replied I had…

… 'And?' she said.

Again, all I could write was… 'I am'…

'We will talk when I'm home,' she replied… I still can't remember the film we watched at the cinema that night, but I do remember sobbing into Dan's shoulder, like ugly, snotty nose, screwed-up face sobbing, while he just held me and reassured me, he wasn't going anywhere.

I can't remember talking to my mum about it, but I do remember her asking me what I wanted to do and her saying, 'We better meet this Dan then.'

I remember my auntie standing in my mum's kitchen, saying, 'I know it might be scary, but I know you, Stacey, and you couldn't get rid.' I remember my nan walking in, in tears, telling me my life was over now, and my mum defending me saying it's not over, it's just going to be different. I remember for the first time my dad just holding me; he didn't say a word, he just sighed and held me tight and, in that moment, I felt as though all of those years I felt unloved and unnoticed by him he noticed me then, he felt my fear and he actually cared for me.

I had a relatively straightforward pregnancy with no complications and went into labour on my actual due date: 01.10.09, three weeks before my nineteenth birthday. With the support of Dan and my mum, our beautiful first-born son arrived, weighing 7lb 3oz. He was perfect, which is less than could be said for my now-destroyed foof!

My gorgeous boy had come out with his hand up by his face, which resulted in a third degree tear. Moments after he arrived, I was taken to theatre to have a spinal ready to be stitched back up. After three days in hospital and numerous emotional breakdowns, we were discharged home.

In the early days, I was either sleeping or crying from the exhaustion or the pain and discomfort I was experiencing in the nether regions. I was petrified that Dan was going to leave us because it was bloody hard work and I was hard work. I hated it when he would go out without me as I was adamant that he was still only with me because of the fact I'd had his child. And now I wasn't up to having sex, he was going to get it elsewhere. I'd constantly push him away because of my own insecurities and it nearly cost us our relationship.

The shock of becoming a mum, both physically and mentally, hit me like a bus. The realisation that I could no longer be the spontaneous, carefree teenager I once was held heavy on my heart. But after a few months to readjust, and after lots of reassurance from Dan and support from Mum and Shan, the void I felt was filled with the intense love I had for our boy and the determination to do all I could, to ensure he knew how much he was cared for and had a happy and fulfilled life.

I was determined not to be a stereotypical young mum, to transform the disappointment I knew my family felt into pride that I could still live up to the high expectations they originally had for me. So, although I still wasn't really sure what I wanted to do, when my boy was fifteen months old, I started university to study nursing. It was the easy option; most people with the grades who did a good interview got on the course. It was a well-respected, stable career and proof that being a mum wasn't going to stop me achieving anything.

To begin with I enjoyed it, I loved being around the patients and helping make their days a little brighter, but I hated the hierarchy of the hospital and the conformity of the role. I hated being associated with the shitty care some patients received by those with no compassion or empathy at all. I didn't feel like little old me could make a big enough impact to make a positive change and being the empath that I am it really affected me.

So, when I found out we were expecting again, I was thrilled, knowing I would be taking a break for maternity leave, thinking the space may do me good and I could return with focus and more clarity to finish the last year of my training.

Then during my fifth placement I woke in the night with pains and started to bleed heavily. Not really accepting the fact this could mean anything and not wanting to disturb our first sleeping baby, I tried to sleep hoping that when I woke it would have all been over... little did I know this pregnancy was actually over.

After popping into A&E the following day, still in horrendous pain and bleeding, I was told to do a wee so they could test it. We could hear the nurse on the other side of the door telling the doctor, 'I've got a girl in there thinking she's pregnant, but the test is negative.' She returned, asking me what made me think I was pregnant. Astonished, I replied, 'Well maybe my missed period and the two tests we did that spelled out PREGNANT on them.' The doctor came in and explained our second pregnancy had resulted in a suspected early, complete miscarriage and no further action was required, as I'd now had a negative test result. We were sent on our way.

The indifference that nurse showed us in those moments will forever haunt my mind because regardless of whether I was actually pregnant or not, she should have had the understanding that we thought we were, we had made plans and had expectations for our future as a family of four, sharing our excitement with our close family, and that had all just been taken away.

I felt empty and invisible all over again.

The comments received from those around us, although made with the best intentions, just dug the knife in deeper. All I wanted to do was hug my mum and cry, but she was away with Shan in hospital again, so the only support I had was through a text.

Dan could see I was hurting and tried his best to comfort me, but I don't think he could really understand why I was grieving someone we hadn't even met yet. Nobody understood, and I felt completely alone.

I decided to go back to my training as something to keep me busy and occupied, and I still needed to provide this happy and fulfilled life for Hayden that I'd promised.

A few months later, I began to feel incredibly sick and unwell, my periods still hadn't returned since our suspected miscarriage, so I just put it down to catching some sort of bug on placement. The bug never went. I was back and forth to the GP, who had no explanation as to why I was feeling this way and said to do a test just in case. The thought of going through another miscarriage filled me with absolute dread. The anxiety I felt handing that urine specimen over to the doctor was overwhelming.

'Congratulations! You're pregnant,' he said.

I felt all the feels in that moment: I was speechless and petrified and happy and excited, I couldn't wait to share the news with Dan, but I also didn't want to acknowledge it either, just in case.

It was after our twelve-week scan that showed us we were actually close to sixteen weeks that we decided to announce our second pregnancy.

The moment we found out it was another boy was the moment I decided I did not want to spend any of my time away from this baby and I no longer wanted to miss out on any more time with Hayden pursuing a career that was expected of me, but not one that I was passionate about.

I quit my nurse training and was lucky enough to be a stay-at-home mum.

I loved every second of being with Hayden and, although constantly anxious that something was going to go wrong, I couldn't wait to meet our new addition.

Jensen arrived, and everything was perfect; our first-born had a best friend to grow up with and our family was complete. But everyday worries of getting everything right and the concern I wasn't enough as just a mum started to creep in. I felt something was missing, so I retrained as a beauty therapist to give me something to do around the boys and make me feel less of a failure.

Fast forward three years, ten months after our wedding. Rogan, our honeymoon baby, arrived and from this day I felt completely lost, I'm not going to lie. The jump from two to three babies was tough for me, I lost my identity again in the process of becoming a mum for the third time, I was constantly worried and overwhelmed. I adored these boys, but I felt unfulfilled in being 'just a mum' and this riddled me with guilt and affected all of my relationships. My relationships with my boys and also with Dan because I never felt like I was good enough, as I was, for them.

I felt like a failure and knew we couldn't go on like this.

I decided to delve into the world of personal development and coaching. It was soon after I started that I learned that everything starts with ME.

My past experiences had influenced my beliefs and values.

The relationships I'd previously had had shaped how I viewed myself and, if I wanted anything to change, I had to first change my thoughts.

If I wanted to improve my relationships now, I had to be comfortable with my own company and improve the relationship I had with myself.

To live a life of fulfilment I had to recognise my strengths and ambitions and combine the two.

I realised that I didn't lose myself when I became a mum, it just put me on a path to becoming an improved version of myself and, just because I wanted more than my mum title, didn't mean I wasn't passionate about being a mum too.

It was through lots of personal development, journaling and mindset work that I began to really understand who I was and, by implementing what I had learned into my daily life, I started to see a positive change, not only in myself but in those around me too.

My boys were happier, my marriage was stronger and for once I was proud of being me.

We decided to complete our family with our fourth and final baby and it was during this pregnancy that I decided I had to share what I had learned with all of the other mums that could be feeling like I had: alone, invisible, lost, overwhelmed and anxious, living life on others' terms, depressed by societal expectations and influenced by beliefs formed by others' opinions.

This is when the group *Becoming Mum* was created. It started off as a positive support group. I really wanted it to become a platform to be able to share everything I had learned that had helped me and to coach other women through their own unique journeys. But I still didn't have the belief that little old me could provide enough value, to make a big enough impact on the lives of these other women, who were where I used to be.

It wasn't until our fourth son had to be delivered via emergency section at thirty-two weeks, resuscitated, ventilated and nearly didn't make it that I actually understood the phrase 'life is too short'. This perfect little baby's life was very nearly over before it had even started. I watched as his tiny little body lay there like a little wax doll, all pale and lifeless, covered in wires and tubes, fighting for a chance of survival following a massive foetal maternal haemorrhage.

I prayed that he would make it, promising that, if he did, I'd continue to grow into the best possible woman and mother I could be for him and my other boys and my husband.

I've since then realised my mission is bigger than my limiting beliefs and I have to share what I've learned over the years to help and inspire others.

To ensure that every other mother out there knows how to improve the relationship she has with herself in order to have positive, connected relationships with those she loves.

To show that you can rediscover who you are again, because you are not lost, you just haven't found the right path yet.

To prove that you are not defined by your past experiences.

You are worthy, and you are enough, just as you are.

You can certainly live a life of purpose alongside being an incredible mother.

You do not ever need to feel alone because, like the rest of the amazing women in the book, I'll be the first to say I'm with you, we've been there, we've walked that path and come out the other end. If we can do it, you can too!!

With love, respect and so much kindness, Stacey Matthews, Becoming Mum Xxx

★ ★ ★

Stacey is a twenty-eight-year-old wife to Dan and mumma to four crazy but beautiful little boys. She loves a good cuppa and is a self-confessed journaling addict.

Through personal development, mindset and positive relationship coaching, Stacey helps women rediscover who they are again, after becoming mums!

You can join her and the community of other mummas in the FB group *Becoming Mum:* https://www.facebook.com/groups/537579106592853/

5. Lisa Jane

I was born on Tuesday 24th June 1975 at the William Harvey Hospital in Ashford, Kent, weighing just six pounds and about twenty-two inches long, to my beautiful mum Rosemary and the sperm donor, as he will be known in this. He does not deserve the title of dad! See, he and my mum had got married at an early age. My mum was a nurse and he was a road worker. The thing is, he left my mum when she was three-months pregnant with me! He used to hit her, he was also a womaniser. Fancied himself! LMAO…

We left Ashford when I was three months old and went and stayed with my nanny and grandad on their farm in Sevenoaks, but eventually we moved to a flat in Swanley in 1976. This is where my mum was working as a bar lady and met my dad. I am not going to call him my stepdad as he is my dad. He has done and continues to do for me what my sperm donor couldn't and didn't do. Sperm Donor's own mother, my so-called nan (witch), came to our flat and took the mattress that we slept on and she also contacted social services on my mum for silly reasons. We literally had nothing in that flat! Lots of aggro from the sperm donor, he even turned up at my mum's flat drunk and my dad drove him home to the witch. You see, my mum and I were the black sheep of the family in the witch's eyes, her precious son could do no wrong.

We soon moved in together with my dad into a two-up, two-down little house along the main road and my dad's dad and stepmum had their family flooring shop, which my mum started to work in. They got married in 1978, not long after my brother was born. Growing up was easy, or so I thought. Primary school was great. I had started dancing and Brownies and loved it. I also remember that feeling of something being different.

36

I couldn't put my finger on it, but it was always there in the back of my mind.

Secondary school was horrific for me. This is where the bullying started, the name-calling, the feeling of no one liking me. I was too skinny, they didn't like the colour of my mum's skin or mine for that matter. I had some lovely friends in secondary school and we still keep in touch now, but I will always remember the bullies and the name-calling, as that is what sticks in my mind.

Thank goodness I had my dancing, which kept me busy, and I was virtually dancing every day of the week. I was damned good at it and I loved dancing with a passion, especially ballet and modern. I was the youngest in my ballet class and just loved to learn the dances and do the exams. I was put in for a lot of shows all over the south of the country as a solo dancer. My mum drove me to them and my dad paid for all the dancing stuff; outfits, shoes, exam fees, etc. Watching me dance was not his thing! Lol.

I soon started helping my teacher in her classes before mine, just so I could dance. The buzz of just dancing was my life. I remember at some point in my teens the usual arguments with your parents, the stomping upstairs and blasting the music out; I loved my music too, lol. I had got it into my head that one day I would find the sperm donor just to find out why he just left me, it was always nagging at me.

Somewhere in between, I did find my sperm donor. He had remarried, and his wife was heavily pregnant when I met them. It was a strange feeling, as I knew that he knew that I knew what he had done to my mum all those years ago. My sister came along, and I got very close to both my sister and her mum. I used to stay there, and she treated me like her own. I also remember being there when he kicked off at her, calling her lazy and a bad mum. I remember shouting at him, 'This is exactly what you done to my mum and now you're just going to do the same to my little sister…' I got the blame for him having a supposedly nervous breakdown and I say it like that as he was and probably still is a compulsive liar. I kept in touch with my little sister and her mum, but distance was a big issue… I never saw the sperm donor after those couple of years.

I eventually gave dance up as, being in the adult world, it just didn't fit anymore. I started working in London for a Korean firm. I will never forget my first pay cheque. It was made out to Miss Risa instead of Lisa. Made me chuckle for ages. I loved working for them, but they soon went bust. I had to find another job, which luckily I did in an architecture company. Still in London.

Somewhere in between, I met this lad eight years older than me; I had just turned eighteen! He was painting my friend's house and it was just a bit of banter and then we started seeing each other. You see, he was like a bad boy, you know, the ones your mums tell you not to get involved with! Well, guess what, I got involved with him, which my parents didn't like, but still supported me anyway. I soon moved out of home to a scummy flat in Walthamstow. I hated it. Travelling to and from work was a risk in itself. We hardly had anything furniture-wise, let alone money-wise, sometimes sitting in the dark. He was always out with his mates. I eventually decided enough was enough and needed to move back to Kent, but decided to get a mortgage. I found out at a later stage that he couldn't get one as he already had one with his ex-partner. First I had heard of this. So, I stupidly got a mortgage in just my name. It was a two-bed maisonette, needed some work doing to it, and I thought we could get it all sorted out. We moved in and things were okay. He was often out or at work, and often in the pub! Little to my knowledge, while I was working a full-time job in London with an hour's journey there and back!

I fell pregnant at the age of twenty. I was shocked, happy, excited, nervous and very scared. Especially telling my dad. It didn't go down too well, but both my parents supported me. Still travelling to and from London was doing me in, especially with the awful sickness that the pregnancy brought with it. I had to be signed off work for ages. My work colleagues were all like 'you are far too young to settle down and have kids' and I was like 'this is what life is all about'.

Eventually, my maternity leave came and they bought us some lovely gifts to start our young family off. This is where I saw his mask slip. The drinking got worse, the gambling got worse and I didn't realise at the time he was on drugs. I had saved up about £600, which was a struggle with trying to pay the bills and the mortgage on my own, but I was really pleased and wanted to go and get the baby a cot and buggy, only to discover he had gambled my money away, which was for his baby too. He started coming in at all hours and it would be 'oh you look fat, you look tired, you look ill'… eerrr, hello, I am heavily pregnant, you realise! One day, laying on the sofa, I couldn't feel the baby move. I called the midwife who came round and we eventually found the heartbeat, but she was concerned that the baby was not moving. I was sent to hospital to be monitored. A few days later, I had to go for a sweep, bearing in mind I was only young and had no clue what that was. All I remember is this big black doctor coming in and putting one of those surgical gloves on and, as he did that, he spread his hand… I was like 'where is that going?' He said, 'I have to have a feel up there!' I was mortified; as if you're gonna get that massive hand up there! His response was 'you are having something much bigger than my hand to worry about soon'! Lol.

I was in labour for ages with my first born and, to be totally honest, I do not remember much of the labour or the birth as I had had pethadine. I remember the baby being put on my chest and him crying. I had this tiny bundle in my arms and no fucking clue what to do or how to do it… then the news came… he was born with club foot. The surgical name is talipes. For those that do not know what this is, it's a birth defect where one or both feet are rotated inwards and downwards. The affected foot, calf and leg may be smaller than the other. In about half of those affected, both feet are involved. Both his feet were affected, his right one was by far the worst! We were told it was hereditary too and that as his was so severe he might not walk. Blow after blow kept coming and that's when the ex really ramped up his game.

I had to ring my sperm donor and ask if there was anything he wanted to tell me, after my mum had said that his dad had it. I remember saying to him that I had given birth to a boy and that he was born with club foot and did anyone in the family have it. He didn't even say congratulations on the birth and told me 'nope, don't know' and put the phone down. His own father was born with it! Well, as you can imagine, the baby blues came. I was being told by my partner that this was all my fault and his drinking and drug-taking got worse.

At six weeks old, my son had his first operation and both his legs were in tiny plaster casts. I remember it was snowing and had settled and his plaster was slipping off his worst leg. I needed to get him back to the hospital. As usual, my partner was nowhere to be seen. I rang the pub only to be told he wasn't there. I remember walking into the pub and there he was, slumped in the corner, pissed as a fart. A lady opposite us saw me trying to push the pram in the snow and offered to take me back to the hospital. I was forever grateful, and we formed a great friendship.

The little digs, the words coming out from his mouth every time he was drunk, he would verbally abuse me, scream, shout, call me names and would throw things around the place. I tried to keep it tidy and G was such a good baby. We used to get stared at a lot because of his plaster and even one lady accused me of abusing my own son. I broke down in tears in the local café and the lady working there brought me a cup of tea and asked me what was wrong. I told her what the lady had said and told her that actually he was born like it; again, another friendship was made and I still speak to both these ladies now, twenty-odd years down the line. It made me not want to go out at all. It was an awful time for me and I was just so glad I had my mum's full support.

It was our son's first or second birthday and obviously he wanted it in the pub. I gave in as, by this point, he had dragged me down so much just with his words. I started to believe that I looked like a clown with makeup on, I looked like a slag in skirts and dresses and that colour was not my thing, and the verbal abuse was just getting worse and worse. We came home from our son's birthday party and he was as high as a kite on drink and drugs and I just remember him kicking off again, saying that I couldn't be trusted, I was flirting with every man in the pub and honestly that is not me. I was on edge the whole time in the pub as I knew he was watching my every move. I was walking on eggshells and didn't really realise that I was. I just remember thinking it was all my fault and that if I behaved and did as I was told, things would get better. On my own, I got our son into Great Ormond Street hospital where he had a further two operations and all the time he was taking the glory for it all. We would stay at his mum's house and he would just sit there all night getting drunk or out and about with his mates on drugs. The fights and the arguments he and his sisters had were an eye-opener and very scary.

Things got worse and he started throwing more things, taking lightbulbs out and even locked me in the bathroom once. I just kept thinking 'I can make this all better'. I fell pregnant with our second baby and was reminded on a daily basis that if this one was born with a deformity, I would know about it. Like I didn't already know about it! I was petrified throughout the second pregnancy and kept asking for scans, but no, thankfully, our second son was born all okay.

That still wasn't good enough. See, the second son was a screamer, didn't sleep. Was up all night with really bad colic and my partner just didn't understand or help. Literally every night he would be drunk. I started smoking weed just to block him out. Only a little, but enough to block the abuse. One night, J was screaming really badly and had woken him and our first son up. He didn't help me, he just screamed and shouted at me to sort the fucking kids out or he would. I was petrified trying to sort out a screaming baby and a three-year-old toddler on my own. I managed to get G back to bed and settled, all the while thinking he was looking after J. I came down to see the window wide open and he was sitting on the window ledge with J in his arms. He was gesturing to throwing J out of the window.

It carried on like this for a couple more years. A few friends had seen and heard for themselves how he was treating me and then the words 'domestic violence' kept popping up in conversations. I was even timed doing the nursery run and then the school run. He went to punch me one day while I was holding J. Luckily, I moved quicker than his fist and he ended up punching a tiled wall. He had broken four of his knuckles. So that just shows how hard that punch was. He had to have an operation and, as usual, I was there; he promised he would change. How many times had I heard that now? I honestly thought this had to be the last time.

He came home, and things were good for a little while, until one day I was washing up and he grabbed me from behind by my throat. Apparently one of his drunks had seen me talking to a man on the school run… the screaming, the shouting was endless. I was cowering in the corner asking to go to the boys, as both of them had heard and seen this and run straight upstairs to their room. He left. I could go to the boys. I settled them and then it was just a matter of time as to when he would be back and what my punishment would be this time.

I had to get up in the night to get J a bottle. I walked into my front room with him and five strange men sleeping. All you could see was vodka bottles and lines of coke on the table. I quickly made the bottle and ran back upstairs. Little did I know that I had woken him up. Yet again, the screaming, the shouting, the poking, the slaps came, and a whole lot worse. Something had to change, but I didn't know who to talk to. I was so ashamed as people close to me told me what was happening and I kept standing up for him to them.

Then that day came. I was just leaving for the school run and, to this day, I do not know what started him off. G was five and at school and J was just two. He came flying at me, pinned me up by my throat with a knife to it and, in front of the boys, he told them, 'You don't call her Mummy, you call her Cunt,' which was a name I got called regularly. I don't know how I got out of there, but I did, and I remember ringing my mum and asking for help.

That was 26th September 2001. That day changed my life forever. The police were called, and I had to go to them with the boys in what we stood in. We were put into a women's refuge, away from my friends and family, and I knew that the gossip would just get worse now. We arrived at this refuge and, well, it was not the nicest of places. I do remember ringing my sperm donor up to say what had happened as he had a tendency to just turn up at my doorstep, and his words have stayed with me all these years. His response was 'oh history repeating itself'! I had to put the phone down.

We were so scared, and I knew I had to be strong for the boys… the nightmare was different, but still there, if that makes sense. I had to go to the benefits office and they refused to help me, all because I had £3.78 in my bank account! Like, what the actual feck can you get with that?! I needed everything from nappies and milk to clothes and necessities like food.

We spent six to seven weeks in that place. I remember a lady was in there with her two children and she told me to lock ourselves in at night and if we were in during the day to stick to ourselves. There were about six women in there and all handled things differently. There were rules that we had to abide by too. I remember being woken up by this awful screaming and children crying. I had to settle my boys and eventually plucked up the courage to go and see what was happening. The lady that helped me on my first day had tried to take her own life in front of her children. I was mortified as I was thinking I couldn't cope and wanted to end it all, but after seeing and hearing it all I eventually came to the conclusion that I had to do this, not for me but for my boys. They are my life and I will do whatever it takes. After seeing that, I had to do this, I had to fight every step of the way.

First fight was to get back into my own house as I owned it on my own. First court case and I got the order to get him to leave. Second fight was the boys. I honestly didn't want them to have anything to do with him after everything that had happened. G had started wetting the bed and J had a stammer, and they both had behavioural problems, which I will add now soon settled. In court, I remember the judge ordering a drugs test as he had told them I was a druggie... like, who the fuck do you think you are?! So, the judge ordered a full blood and hair strand test for both of us and low and behold he had a full body wax. Not one bit of hair left on his body.

The judge ordered that he could come back into the family home for contact. I had to agree for the boys' sake. It was so stressful for me and the boys, as I would lock myself in my bedroom. The verbal abuse started soon after and then he would sit in his car all night at the bottom of my road and just flash his lights at my house so I knew he was there. The police couldn't/wouldn't do anything.

I finally got help from the school with the boys' behaviour and we went and got counselling, which did help the boys, thankfully. I tried to shield them from a lot, as the abuse and the threatening behaviour from him was just relentless. I did tell the boys' counsellor that the arrangements were not working and that I would agree to a contact centre, as I couldn't cope with it all; the stress, the anxiety and the depression just took over me. I agreed to every other weekend and every other Christmas, which worked pretty well for a few years, until I met my now husband S. The threats all started back up and got even worse when I was pregnant and then had my daughter, to the point that my eldest mentioned at his house about his little sister and he was dropped off on the motorway. So much has gone on that I cannot possible tell you. A few years passed...

Then one day I kept seeing this advert for 3D mascara. I signed up, not knowing anything about makeup or the company. I received my kit and just left it at that… all the while still seeing all these posts. I dug into the company more and realised their mission behind it is to help women and children who have been abused. BOOM, I knew then that this was for me. I was told about mindset and personal development and thought 'what load of crap'! I kept seeing it and seeing it and thought 'okay, Lis, you have to have a look into this more'. Well, WOWZERS, what a difference. For me, personally, it has really helped me change my mindset and my attitude towards life and other things like my anxiety and depression. How I handle situations and feelings now is totally different to what I say would be the old me. It has also given me back my confidence and I absolutely love helping other women too. I am now enjoying wearing makeup again and learning all about skincare and how to help others learn and grow. My journey is just beginning, but most importantly showing my daughter that you can be whoever you want to be, not what society tells you you have to be.

★ ★ ★

Lisa Jane is forty-three years old and lives with her husband Steve in Kent. She is a very proud mum to G, J and L and also a proud nanny to M. Lisa Jane has a passion for uplifting, validating and empowering women through makeup and skincare, and loves supporting other mums in business.

www.instagram.com/lusciousbossbabes

6. Jen

Throughout my childhood I only ever dreamed of one career. From my childhood invisible friend called PC Pinkerton, playing detectives with my older brother and our toy sets that included magnifying glasses and real fingerprint powder, through to my subject choices at university, I only ever wanted to join the police force. I had visions of working my way up through the force, from a PC through to a detective, and of being the youngest woman ever to grace the biggest board tables in the country!

I have very fond memories of my childhood; overall it was happy. It was not without its difficulties, however, but whose is? My brother and I were pretty well behaved, other than the usual sibling squabbles, and that is testament to our incredible mum. I remember the day the tough part of my childhood began very well. I came home from my first day of year six, excited because it was my best friend's birthday, only to find my mum running around the house in a frenzy, picking up the phone and making phone calls and seeming to panic. My dad had left. As the days went on, although she did her best to hide it from us, I saw my mum upset like I never had before, which was incredibly difficult to see. Dad had met someone else and had ended their relationship.

Or so we thought. What was to become harder than him leaving was the fact that it didn't just end there. They would get back together and the possessions would slowly move back in – only to drift back out of the door again. Difficult weeks turned into difficult months, which turned into difficult years. I had to witness my mum cope with the emotional trauma on a long-term basis, battling depression, all the while trying to keep it hidden from my brother and I – although that was impossible –

and trying to cope with an incredibly hard situation on her own. Despite the upsetting memories of this time for me, there were many positives too. We had some amazing adventures, just the three of us, such as coach trips to Italy and even Poland! All of this taught me how important strength, resilience, determination and selflessness are, which has become even more important in starting my own business and becoming a mum myself.

During this time, my health came under question. It started at the end of primary school when, having always been an active child – playing the usual games in the playground, doing handstands against the school walls, cartwheels on the field and playing leapfrog – I started to find certain things difficult due to stiffness and pain in my joints; in particular, in my hips and my knees. I started to struggle to sit with my legs crossed in assemblies and was no longer able to play leapfrog like I could just a few months before. My mum took me to the GP about it a fair few times, but it was put down to 'growing pains'. It got worse during secondary school and I was sent to physiotherapy where we were told that my legs had grown too quickly for the muscles, meaning that the bones had grown twisted and the shortened muscles were what were causing it to feel like my hips were popping out of joint when I walked. I had lots of physiotherapy and hydrotherapy, but it got to the point where it wasn't making much difference and the only option was surgery. We were told that I'd be in plaster from my middle right down to my toes for one leg at a time for months on end, with very little chance of success. With hindsight, I'm really pleased we made the decision not to go with this option, as it proved it would have been a fruitless exercise!

During my teens I kept fit and active, so that although I still had joint issues, I ploughed on and tried not to let it bother me, thinking it was all in my head. I loved sports and, again with hindsight, this probably stopped my problems from getting a lot worse at the time. I struggled with mental health problems too, all centring around control, which was understandable given the surrounding family and health issues that I couldn't do anything about. I controlled my calorie intake to an excessive degree, not necessarily to lose weight (although I wasn't displeased with this side effect, which I wrongly thought I hid well under baggy clothes), but more to feel like I had control over something. It also manifested itself in sleep disorders, with bad dreams, sleepwalking and night terrors.

My first job was at sixteen as a waitress in a café. I loved this job. However, it didn't last very long because of my joint issues. It grew increasingly difficult to carry massive oval platters filled to the brim with full English breakfasts in each hand because my wrists would hurt so much, and trying to lift the heavily-loaded tray of dishes from inside the dishwasher to the top of it, in order to load a fresh tray, hurt my back and my hips so much I could no longer do it. I had to leave after just a few months. It was a huge blow to my confidence because I felt like I must be weak to not be able to do the tasks girls half my size seemed to have no issues doing.

When I was seventeen, I got a job behind the bar in my local village pub. This was a real eye-opener. As a shy, slightly awkward teenager who blushed any time a stranger said my name, I suddenly had to pull pints, cope with pub banter, remember drinks and specific glasses for each of the regulars, all with a smile on my face. That, combined with my increasing interest in my drama classes at school, meant I quickly learnt to come out of my shell and give as good as I got. I learnt that the more I could have a laugh with the locals and make the restaurant visitors feel comfortable, the more tips I got, plus the more I enjoyed my job.

However, my back caused me more and more problems. I worked every school holiday and every break from university and I found that if I did several split shifts in a row, I would finish the night having to crouch down with my burning hot back against the fridge to cool it down and ease the pain. *But everyone gets back pain, right?* That's what I thought. I would wake up incredibly stiff and sore, but found that moving helped ease this off, so as long as I got going relatively quickly then I was okay. Nothing to worry about!

It was during this time that my mum and dad's relationship finally ended for good. He was having a baby with his girlfriend and that was the end of that; he was making a fresh start with a new family and my mum was having a clean break. It was the best thing that could have happened to both of them. My baby brother is now turning into an incredible young man. My dad had his own company when he was born, whereas with me and my older brother he had a job that meant he worked away most of the time. The utter devastation I felt as a child when he was going to yet another conference at Disneyworld (Microsoft had the best conferences, as far as I was concerned!) means that a trip there is firmly on my vision board! Working from home meant he got to spend a lot more time with his third child and had a much more primary role in his upbringing. This is part of the inspiration behind me wanting a career that I can balance much more easily with raising my children. My mum, on the other hand, threw herself into work. She had four part-time jobs at one point. She was a teacher, a secretary and a driving instructor – and she even took a couple of shifts in the same pub as me. This was partly to distract herself from her relationship ending, but also because she wanted to support my brother and I through university. I couldn't be more grateful for this support, and her sheer determination to do everything that she was doing was incredibly inspiring. It was also a lot of fun when our shifts at the pub coincided! It also inspired me because I never wanted to be in that situation – meaning a healthy work-life balance became even more important to me.

I love the English language and so it made sense for me to choose to study it at university. I learned about sentence structure, the meaning of sentences, differences in speech and dialect and the origins of the English language. I learnt analytical skills and developed a true passion. I didn't want it to end when my three years were up, so I continued at the same university with an MSc in Forensic Speech Science, studying how language can be used in criminal cases, such as comparing the voice and speech patterns in a criminal recording with that of a suspect to see how similar they are and how likely they are the same person. It wasn't like *CSI,* where you put the speech into a machine and it gives you a magical definitive answer; this was laborious analysis by a human to find the similarities and differences. I loved it and couldn't wait to put it into practice in my career once I had finished university.

The joint problems continued, but I kept fit and active, mainly so I could eat and drink what I liked without gaining weight! Towards the end of my Masters, my fourth finger and thumb on my right hand kept swelling up, which I put down to repetitive strain injury from writing so much during my studies. I was also under a lot of stress during this final year from outside forces. My gran died in the December of my final year. Not long after that, my mum got diagnosed with breast cancer. It was horrendous being so far away while she was dealing with this, but my brother was a brilliant support to her during this time. She ended up having a mastectomy, her lymph nodes under one arm removed, chemotherapy and radiotherapy. She is a Scouser and hard as nails, so it didn't surprise me how well she coped with all of this!

Having promised myself I would throw myself into my studies, concentrate on me and get an amazing degree, followed by a year travelling round the world with my best friend, things started to change in the very first week of the first term when I met my now-husband! He also had plans to travel the world with his best friend after university, so by the end of that year we were all arranging to travel together. And so, after my mum was given the initial all-clear from her cancer, we did. My bestie had to cut her trip short, leaving me with the boys – and in that time my joints had got progressively worse. My bestie is a lot smaller than me, and so I felt incredibly weak when I struggled to lift and carry my backpack, whilst she appeared to have no problems. As the weeks went on at the start of our travels around south-east Asia, I struggled more and more, needing help to get my backpack on and off my back. My back pain was excruciating, and my swollen finger and thumb got more and more painful. By the time we got to Thailand I couldn't straighten my right hand flat or make it into a fist. I had to have help getting my wetsuit on when we learnt to scuba dive and had to be hoisted back onto the boat every time because I couldn't make it up the ladder. Was I that unfit?!

My swollen fingers looked like they might have an infection, so I went to the doctor as soon as we landed in Australia. He took one look at them and said, "I know what it is and you're not going to like it!" I was shocked that he referred me to a rheumatologist, and I went to see him in just five days. I thought he couldn't possibly be right that the problem was rheumatological. My job for the few months just before travelling was a shared reception job with a lady who suffered from rheumatoid arthritis, and she was really disabled. I didn't struggle as much as her, so it couldn't possibly be right. However, the specialist did lots of tests, took lots of measurements and asked me a lot of questions. We discussed all my aches and pains that I had assumed were normal. He discovered that my pain and stiffness was worse in the morning when waking up, but would ease off with exercise, unless I overdid it, which would make the pain worse. But everyone is stiff when they wake up, right?

Wrong. I was diagnosed with ankylosing spondylitis, which causes inflammation of the joints in the spine and pelvis, as well as swelling in soft tissue. It's an autoimmune disease; the immune system mistakenly thinks there is a problem in the joints and sends white blood cells, attacking the healthy tissue and causing swelling, stiffness and pain. A clear marker is a raised white blood cell count, as well as stiffness and pain in the mornings. I also got diagnosed with psoriatic arthritis, which is in the same family but causes issues with the extremities, such as fingers and toes, plus includes the skin condition psoriasis. It was made clear that these weren't problems that would go away; it was a lifetime condition that could be managed with medication and exercise but that couldn't be cured. I remember walking out of his office in a daze, not knowing where to go or what to think. In a nearby park, I called my mum. I longed to be home and not have to deal with this on the other side of the world.

Our two-week stop in Perth had to be extended so that the rheumatologist could get my condition under control as much as possible before we continued our trip. Despite me telling them to continue without me, the boys stayed with me and were an incredible support during a difficult time. They put up with a lot, as the steroids I was on gave me severe mood swings, plus caused rapid weight gain. I couldn't have got through that time without them and I am incredibly grateful. We got jobs and lived in a little house together for eight months. I ended up on injections to suppress my immune system and started feeling healthy again, so I was given the all-clear and enough medication to get me through the rest of the trip. There were several times when I wanted to give up and just fly home, but persevered, with the help of my now-husband and his best friend supporting me, as well as family back home. The rest of the trip was incredible, and we had amazing experiences that I hope to share in my writing at some point in the future! But we did have to change our plans, not visiting as many places as planned in Australia and spending far less time in subsequent countries. I also wasn't allowed to drink with my medication, so I had to step back from the party side of travelling.

I returned home a different person. I had grown so much through my experiences and was determined not to let my diagnosis affect my life negatively. However, when I applied to join the police, I was shocked to find that they wouldn't even let me get past the first stage of the application process. The question was: 'Do you have an autoimmune disease such as rheumatoid arthritis?' and I had to tick 'Yes'. I wasn't allowed to progress any further and my dream career was in tatters. So, what was I to do? I applied for every job that even slightly interested me, which at the time were mostly admin jobs because of my work experience. Two interviews stood out for me. One was as an office manager on a good salary, but with only two people in the office and no room for progression. The other was with a publishing house, lower on the ladder and less money, but with room for progression into a potential career that I could really get on board with. My love of language naturally gave me a love of books, and I had always been an avid reader. And so, my career began.

I started off picking and packing book orders in the warehouse, stuffing envelopes for the marketing department and doing general admin for the company, but the side to my job that I enjoyed most was the work I did for the production department. Initially just making proof corrections to text, I progressed to typesetting (designing text to make it look like a professionally published book), then handling my own authors and designing book covers. I ended up as Group Production Manager, managing the design teams across all of the company's different imprints. I absolutely loved my work, but it involved long hours and high stress levels, which naturally took a toll on my health. By this point I had an extra diagnosis of fibromyalgia (which causes inflammation and pain in the muscles). The immunosuppressants I was on to treat my conditions meant I was frequently coming down with the slightest bug that was brought into the office and pushed round the air-conditioning system, and I was struggling with extreme fatigue. One of the biggest challenges of working in an office with chronic illness and disability was time off. The company I worked for did everything by the book, and I couldn't complain about how they handled anything professionally, but the procedures meant that it was extremely difficult for me to cope at times. I came down with an awful virus early on in my production career that made it almost impossible just to get out of bed and I just wanted to sleep all day. The GP prescribed bed rest, as that's all they could do, but it meant missing a couple of weeks of work. This virus knocked me, and for several months I came down with the slightest thing. I lost my voice several times (one time for thirteen weeks, needing speech therapy to get it back!) and I was off work regularly. It got to the point where every time I was back in the office I had to go into a meeting with one of the managing directors and my head of department and it felt humiliating having to explain my time off every time, even though it was standard procedure when someone had more time off sick than normal. I frequently got upset, feeling like I was letting colleagues and clients down, and like I was constantly trying to catch up. I got stressed about getting ill, which made me run down, meaning I had to go through that even more. It was a vicious cycle. Although professionally accepted, personally those procedures did more harm than good, and the mental health side of chronic illness needs to be researched more in terms of keeping staff in the workplace.

My life became all work and no play.

Well, not all work! I got married in 2015; it was one of the best days of my life, even with the extra worry of my mum being diagnosed with cancer for the second time not long before we tied the knot. We had a house and a puppy (Doug was a special guest at the wedding!) and, after we married, decided to try for a baby. I had to stop my medication six months before we could start trying. Luckily, I fell pregnant in four months, but ten months without medication was incredibly difficult. However, pregnancy made me feel better than any medication. I got healthier, despite being overweight when I got pregnant, and I got in better and better shape the further I got into my pregnancy. I could walk the dog further and I was happier than I had been in a long time. When my beautiful daughter arrived in October 2016, everyone commented on how happy I seemed; motherhood obviously suited me. The truth was, I was more relaxed than I had been in a long time, which with a newborn is a pretty mean feat. Stress was a major factor in making it harder to cope with my arthritis. As my maternity leave progressed, I started to get anxious about returning to work. So, after conversations with my family and my employer, I made the decision to go freelance. My employer was incredibly supportive and really helped me to start out on my own. I started my company, Fuzzy Flamingo (the name is for another story!), in September 2017 providing editing and design services. During the whole of my publishing career I had been a freelance editor alongside my job and so it was a great way to start the company, with projects from my publisher. During this time, I developed my design skills, doing more courses and expanding my portfolio from books to marketing materials, stationery, logos and branding. I then officially launched the design side in January 2018 and I haven't looked back!

My home office is adapted to my needs. My desk raises and lowers so I can work standing or sitting. I have a coccyx cushion that supports how I sit, whilst relieving the pressure on my spine; a footrest; a chair that moves in every way possible to get to the perfect supportive position; and everything is easily accessible on my desk. I take breaks whenever necessary, I can walk my dog whenever I start to get too stiff, and I can spend more time with my daughter. Starting my own company would not have been possible without the support of my husband, the inspiration from my mum and dad, nor without finding the fantastic support network I have with the Mums in Business Association. I'm the official editor, typesetter and ebook formatter for their *Mumpreneur on Fire* series, starting with book three; I've been a guest speaker at a MIBA networking event, and am hoping to do more talks with them and other companies in the future, as this is something I love doing. I've had amazing design clients, created logos, branding and more that I'm really proud of, more than one publisher on board when it comes to the editing side and I'm doing better than I ever thought possible with social media marketing! I didn't even have an Instagram account before I started my business.

I am a finalist for awards that will be announced at ceremonies at the beginning of next year and I cannot wait to see what's around the corner – including my second baby, who is due in December! My mum continues to be an inspiration, battling cancer for the third time, but in her words: "Don't let the b★★tards get you down!" She is proof that life is too short; you need to enjoy every moment and go for what you want in life. Get that vision board up and get working towards it!

I would like to leave you with this thought from C.S. Lewis: "There are far, far better things ahead than any we leave behind." I may have thought my dream was to be in the police, but in having that door closed I had several opened that are even better! Don't give up if things aren't working. Change directions and you might just find yourself looking at a better view.

★ ★ ★

Jen Parker is thirty-two and lives in Leicester with her husband, daughters and pooch. She also lives with autoimmune disease. Jen is a freelance graphic designer and editor with her own company, Fuzzy Flamingo. With a background in publishing, Jen specialises in book design (covers and text) and small business branding, working with self-publishing authors, publishing houses and business owners. She is also a copyeditor and proofreader, working with publishers, authors, business owners and bloggers. You can find her on Instagram and Facebook by searching for FuzzyFlamingoDesign.

Get behind the scenes access, hints and tips in Jen's blog on her website: www.fuzzyflamingo.co.uk.

7. Michelle C

My story isn't that different from many growing up in a middle-class family in the suburbs of Chicago. Unfortunately, 3000 words isn't nearly long enough to go into the self-loathing I went through as a teenager as I was seeking attention in all the wrong places to provide me the approval I so desperately wanted. I look back now mortified of the person I was and pray my daughter doesn't go down the same destructive path. Luckily, I had enough sense to dig my way out. Even after being raped by a boyfriend, almost being raped by a friend of a friend, sexually harassed and assaulted in almost every job I've been in. The sad thing is, this will be the first time my parents and everyone apart from a few close friends and my husband will be hearing about it. The way of the world is to shut your mouth and move on with your life. If you talk about it, you let it happen, you are weak, and it's your fault. Instead of the fault of the perpetrator that thinks they can do whatever they want as they are in a position of power or because telling me that they have a Prince Albert piercing they would like to show me is an appropriate way to ask me out on a date. Or the numerous men who use online dating as the new bar scene and expect after buying me dinner that I need to pay them back by getting on my knees.

There are not enough words to describe how it feels when you find your light in the darkness. When you find that person who is with you despite your past, despite how it still affects you in the present. There are not enough words to describe how I felt giving birth to my two amazing children, or their surgeries, illnesses, or my first miscarriage. But there are enough words to share the turning point in my life and how you too can find the light. It doesn't matter how long you've been in the dark, you can always find the light.

My name is Michelle and in thirty-two years of life some really bad shit has happened to me. The other twenty-four women in this book will have their own shitty experiences that dragged them down to the depths of hell. But what people didn't expect was that we would find our way out, better, stronger and much, much wiser. You might have kept us quiet for countless years. You may or may not be the reason we have suffered in silence with PTSD, anxiety, depression and countless other issues. But together, we are strong, together we are fighting back to prove we cannot be silenced, we cannot be stopped. Together we are showing other women, our daughters, future generations to never give up. To keep fighting through the tears, as they are worth so much more than they know. Together, we are mumpreneurs, so sit back and listen to our words, because we are on fire!

May 2018

The tears were flowing freely as I got the news, my baby didn't have a heartbeat. I was supposed to be eight weeks along, but the baby was only measuring five weeks and five days. I was devastated, empty; how could this be happening again?! It took me a whole year to fall pregnant again, after my first miscarriage, and now the joy of making my family complete was being stripped away from me. Only three weeks earlier I was diagnosed with Ankylosing Spondylitis, an autoimmune disease that causes chronic pain and arthritis in your back and joints. They say bad things come in threes and if this was what the first two were, I was petrified for the third. The rest of the day I was on autopilot, just going through the motions, but never really present and I thought, 'How did I get to this place?'

September 2009

I only had a week until I was due to fly to London to start my Master's degree and I still had no place to live and no money until my student loan came through six weeks after my course started. I was fortunate enough to have a family friend to use their miles to get me a ticket from Chicago to London, and my Student Work Visa had come through a couple of weeks earlier. I now needed to secure enough money to find a place to stay while I searched for a permanent place to live, as well as expenses. Through talking to everyone I knew and a written promise to return the borrowed funds, I was lent enough money to get a hotel for a week and living expenses. I wouldn't realise it now, but my mind was so focused on getting to England that I manifested everything that was happening with the Universe.

Over that week I had to pack up my life into suitcases for the most thrilling and scary adventure of my life; I was moving to a new country on my own, where I knew no one. I did have some friends that I had met a year earlier who were doing an exchange program for football, but all in all, I was well and truly alone for the first time in twenty-two years.

The morning when I boarded the plane and said bye to everyone and everything I knew, I was full of good butterflies; you know the kind, tingles from your head to your toes when you step into the unknown, but deep down you know it's going to be spectacular. I will never forget looking out of the window as we circled around London before landing. The orange lights of the M25 and Heathrow, the muted sky as we descended through the clouds and approached the landing strip, the screeching brakes as we halted to a stop in Terminal 3, all of these things are forever etched into my memory as the first day of the rest of my life.

The first few weeks were rough as I adjusted to life on my own and in a different country. I found a place to live with one of those friends doing their exchange program. Their mother generously rented out their spare room to me, so I could have an affordable place to live. It did mean me travelling into London three days a week for school, but I still saved money by not living in the city.

I made friends in the area, but not many at school as I was really only there for my classes and in the library or computer lab. The first six weeks flew by, but then I was terribly homesick. I felt vulnerable and lost, that none of these 'friends' I made were really my own. As sad as this might have made my mother, I know she was secretly ecstatic as we scrambled together some money to send me home for Christmas.

Once again, without knowing it, we manifested the funds to send me home the day after Christmas for ten days. Knowing I was going to be home, going back to people that were truly mine, put me at ease for the remainder of my first term at school.

December 2009

As Christmas crept into the air, I thought I would treat myself to a Christmas present of going on online dating. Now, when I tried online dating back in the States it was a succession of horrible dates, scumbags and stomach-wrenching experiences, but I thought to myself 'not every guy is a douchebag, right?' I went on my first date with a nice guy a few days before Christmas. My papers were all submitted and I was done with school until late January, so felt relaxed and excited about going home and the tingling you get when you meet someone new.

We had a lot of fun, but at the end of it, I felt he was more of a friend than boyfriend material. We chatted a little after that but decided not to take it further. I still checked my profile occasionally but was immersed into a completely different world of Christmas that I had never experienced before. British traditions are very different to what I was used to growing up and it was such a wonderful thing to be a part of, especially knowing I would still get that Christmas feel back at home.

It was Boxing Day and I was heading back to Chicago to be with my friends and family that I so desperately needed. I needed that reassurance of who I was, and that it was natural for me to feel homesick even though I was so lucky to be studying in a different country. I needed a mental and emotional MOT and being home did that for me. While I was home, I started getting messages from this guy from the online dating site. He seemed really charming and genuine. He would send me really long messages and I would only send direct responses back; oddly I never elaborated much, but we kept talking. Eventually, we made plans to meet up when I returned back to England. Suddenly, being in a foreign country on my own didn't seem so lonely.

January 2010

I arrived back to those burning orange lights of Heathrow on the 8th of January. I was due to start my job the next day, so was wasting no time getting back into the swing of things. As soon as I was able, I quickly texted this new guy to let him know I got home safely, and we had arranged to meet on the 10th. We continued to text (because who talks on the phone these days) all night, and the flutters made it hard to sleep.

The next day I started my new job and, as I worked at a phone store, it was actually okay for me to be on my phone. I was just about to go on my lunch break and I made the leap and asked this guy I had only been talking to for the past week if he wanted to meet for lunch. He apologised as he had already eaten, and was out with his friends, but quickly asked me out for dinner that evening. I was shocked, I thought, 'Wow! This guy must like me, there are good guys out there, he is moving our date to tonight!!'

I don't remember another date like it. Everything was perfect, and we connected on so many levels. When I went home that night, I quickly messaged everyone I knew to say that I had met my husband, seven months later we were engaged and a year after that we got married. Chris has been my biggest support and keeper of my secrets for all these years…

I tell you this because, despite all the crappy things that have happened to me in my life, I regret none of it. I truly believe it was what led me to Chris. When you focus on love, you manifest love, and allow love to come into your life, and once again, without me knowing it, I manifested my perfect partner.

May 2018

This miscarriage affected Chris differently than the first. The first miscarriage was a chemical miscarriage, I didn't even know I was pregnant but around the time my period was due I began to bleed, I bled for sixteen days. I then got an infection in my uterus, so the pain continued, and it affected me deeply, as every day I was bleeding, every day I was in pain or on antibiotics, it was a reminder; whereas Chris, understandably, had a complete disconnect from the situation. But this time it was a lot harder as we knew we were pregnant, and then all of a sudden we weren't. I was carrying my dead child in me for a total of five weeks by the time everything had passed. As the baby was measuring only five weeks and five days they would not do surgery, despite my protest, and instead made me go through the pain of passing the baby naturally. When you want something so badly and then it is taken away from you, all you can think is 'Why me?'

As I mentioned before, I was finally diagnosed with Ankylosing Spondylitis, which I have suffered with for years, but only recently has it become so bad that it was affecting my daily life. I would be so stiff in the morning for hours. Chris would have to help me out of bed, I couldn't bend down to put my socks on and struggled to get the kids dressed. I started to battle with extreme fatigue due to the constant pain and after a year of managing my anxiety, I was having constant panic attacks and struggled to leave the house.

I didn't know what to do, I was losing control after years of trying to feel like myself again as I had Post Natal Depression with my son and it went undiagnosed and untreated for eleven months. I had tried many natural ways to overcome my anxiety but I was drowning and even my medication wasn't working. I had a choice to make: do something drastic to change your mindset and life or be stuck in this never-ending abyss of panic and stress.

Now, I have always seen myself as an optimist and try and see the best in people. My inner voice didn't always say the nicest things to myself, so how could I sit there and tell people to be kind to themselves and how amazing they were if I wasn't believing it myself? I had a mask on to hide my pain and distress and it was time to confront those issues.

July 2018

I made the decision to go to a life coach. It wasn't an easy decision to make as it was much more than a financial investment; it meant confronting and dealing with a lot of suppressed memories, it meant opening up old wounds that would leave me feeling vulnerable. But it was the best decision I have ever made.

We spent nine hours, yes, NINE HOURS doing a full breakthrough. We extracted all of my negative emotions and memories, anything that was holding me back from living my best life. It allowed me to see myself and the world in a different light. I was able to see how some people and things were causing me stress and all I had to do was walk away. We re-associated certain tasks or events from a negative into a positive light and it felt like I was seeing the world for the first time.

I cried. I cried hard, ugly, happy tears. The release of everything that was holding me down was gone, I was weightless. I had spent the last couple of years learning about positive self-development. Reading self-help books, saying affirmations, practicing the law of attraction. But I could finally see why they weren't working. I was only living half a life and didn't embrace everything about myself. From that day I started to live a more grateful life and my world has changed.

I was grateful for the energy shift within me, I was grateful for the negative people that were in my life, as now I could shower them with love and healing, I was grateful for my missteps and failures as it was the Universe showing me a better opportunity. Like a flip of a switch I was in a world of power, control and empowerment. Don't get me wrong, I do have days when I forget to be grateful, when my children, different situations, or that nasty voice in my head gets the better of me. But then I sit back, breathe, recognise those feelings and DECIDE to have a better day.

Living my best life takes work, but it's a decision I make every day to be a better person, I decide to make the most of every day. I still have Ankylosing Spondylitis, the Universe cannot change that, but I can change how I feel about it, I can change how I will let it affect me. It's hard to ignore your pain when it stops you from putting on your own clothes, but I shift my mindset onto what I can do, and that I am seeking the right treatment to make me better. Nothing will happen overnight, but if we decide nothing will change, nothing will.

Every morning you get to decide if it is going to be a good day, or a bad day. You can decide if you're going to be happy, or if you're going to let your troubles overwhelm you. When you focus on the good around you, the positive things in life, you open yourself up to the power of the Universe. You allow positive things to flow into your life. Our thoughts manifest into our reality and I've been living that truth since July and my life has dramatically changed.

If it weren't for these changes, I'd still be struggling with my Network Marketing instead of following my passion to help people realise their true potential. I have been able to rebrand and launch my new business helping people create vision boards to achieve their dreams and desires. We release negativity and invite a positive energy into our life, we use positive affirmations and self-love mantras to remind ourselves how amazing we are. Because I follow a positive light and surrender to the Universe, I've been presented with so many amazing opportunities, like writing in this book, becoming Head Coordinator for North America for MIBA, becoming a presenter on the MIBA retreat, and the wonderful collaborations and clients that have all come from this one simple shift in my life.

I don't expect everyone to run out and go get a life coach, but by practicing gratitude, letting go of the negative thoughts and feelings you are holding on to and giving yourself up to the miraculous possibilities of the Universe, you too can live your best life.

★ ★ ★

Originally from the suburbs of Chicago, Michelle now lives in Leicestershire with her husband, Chris, and her two children, Olivia and Henry. Michelle is a mentor and owner of The Best You helping children and adults be the best version of themselves from the inside out. You can connect with Michelle here:

Facebook: www.facebook.com/groups/THE.BEST.Y0U

8. Emma W

My story starts in secondary school. I hated it. I was bullied, like so many kids are. I was told I was fat, ugly and stupid. I never reached my full potential at school because I could never be myself, I could never relax. I now know that's called a 'reticular hijack'. It means your brain goes into panic mode. It meant my brain wasn't there to learn and thrive, it was just worrying how I'd get through the day (breaks and lunchtimes were the worst). I won't bore you with any more details but it's important to know because it had a massive impact on me then and in my future.

The day I left school was one of elation. I was leaving the bitches behind. I was leaving the hurtful comments behind. But, if you've ever experienced anything similar, you'll know it doesn't stop there.

I may have left the bullies behind, but I took ME with me. I had learnt to believe everything people had said about me. I felt fat, ugly and stupid. My English teacher told me there was no point in doing any A-Levels (what an inspiration she was!). So, I went and worked in my parents' restaurant. They'd always wanted to own a restaurant. It was THE most perfect timing. They bought it the year I finished school. I had no idea what I wanted to do as a job anyway, so it was win-win for everyone.

After a year away from any nasty comments, I came to believe that I could actually do some A-Levels. I only chose two because… you know… I had an ingrained belief that I was stupid, so I'd never be able to manage three. The funny thing is, I learnt that I was actually pretty intelligent. I got better and better grades as I went through the two years at college. My lecturers pleaded with me to take a third A-Level but I decided against it. I took biology and the first (supposedly easier) modules that I took the first term I got Ds. By the end of the course I was getting As on the (quoted by my biology teacher) "harder and more complex" modules. I ended up getting more than enough points to go to university.

I still had no idea what I wanted to do but I'd always loved children, so I followed in my mum's footsteps and trained to be a teacher at Oxford Brookes University.

Fast forward to my first year graduated and working as a teacher in a military school, I found that I was getting constant sore throats and recurrent tonsillitis – this is not unheard of for teachers and so I just put it down to an occupational hazard. I was also not loving it as much as I'd hoped I would.

As the months went by, I thought there must be something wrong with me. I wondered why my job was making me so ill and unhappy. Most of my family and friends found their 'thing' in the form of a job and are very happy and definitely in their 'Zone of Genius'. Unfortunately, that wasn't the case for me. I couldn't understand why I had this longing for something else and why a black cloud hovered over the weekdays but would lift at the weekends.

Although I was graded an outstanding teacher and loved being with the children, I couldn't help but wish for something else. I'd crawl to the weekends and count down the days to the next holiday. I started considering alternatives, but fear and doubt took over. I'd only studied teaching at university. I couldn't think how else I could use my skills. I didn't think I even HAD any other skills.

Plus, I thought starting a business was a 'risk'. So, I ignored the quiet whisper telling me there was something else out there.

By my fourth year teaching, crippling fatigue was starting to consume me and much of my salary was spent trying to regain my health. I'd fall asleep in my pile of books in the middle of marking at 7:30pm. My weekends were spent trying to sleep to build up my battery and planning for the next week. If anyone tells you teachers work nine to three and have it easy because they get thirteen weeks of holiday a year, don't listen to them. That's just the hours with the kids. There are hundreds of additional hours spent each month on top of all that. I'm not work-shy and I loved being with the kids. But it was becoming evident that teaching was not sustainable for me and my health.

I was getting dizzy spells, constantly feeling like I had the flu. I ended up being taken into hospital and two weeks later came out in a wheelchair, diagnosed with Chronic Fatigue Syndrome (CFS). My darkest time was when my sister had to shower me and wash my hair because I didn't have the strength to lift my arms. I'd not long moved into a new home with my then boyfriend and I'd been looking forward to it for months. Yet, I was a shadow of my former self. I remember having to lay on the bed in my new bedroom and watch my parents paint around me because I couldn't lift a paintbrush. It was heartbreaking. I was twenty-five and should have been full of life!

You'd think I'd take stock of this and re-evaluate my life. But nope. I was stubborn and wanted to get back to work and my class as soon as possible.

I knew I had to drastically change my life, but I was terrified. Could I really do something else? I was also terrified that I'd never find anything else that I'd love to do AND get paid any decent money to do it. All those insecurities were rearing their ugly head again. Teaching was my comfort zone and I was good at it.

So yet again, I chose to listen to my fears and went about returning to teaching as soon as I was physically able. I fought hard and tried every pill, potion, diet and technique to help me get well again. I started off teaching a few hours a week and gradually built it up to full-time again.

Funnily enough, I'd found that the way I got through the tough days was to dress in a way that made me feel good. I had one jumper and every time I wore it, people told me I looked well. This made me smile because I felt anything but WELL. However, I realised that it was the COLOUR of the top. It was making me look better. Just as we all have colours that drain us and make us look ill, some colours do the opposite. This fascinated me (I'll come back to this random observation in a bit because it changed my life).

I then got made redundant. Ouch.

I couldn't believe it. This job that I had given my everything to was then ripped from under me.

The thought of finding another school felt wrong. But I didn't know how else I'd pay the bills.

I know why all this happened, though. Like they say – everything happens for a reason. I clearly wasn't going to quit, so life removed my job for me.

I got so sick I ended up unable to look at lights or function properly. That still wasn't enough for me to listen to my body. Once I'd got back to full-time, life swept in and had to do something drastic. I honestly believe that.

At the time, I was utterly devastated. I sobbed myself to sleep for months.

I decided to do supply work, so I could just teach three days a week and regain my strength so I wasn't a washout by the weekend. I wanted to have a LIFE not just a job.

With that extra space in my life, I had time to think. Something I never did before. I always kept myself busy, so it never felt like I knew who I was outside of teaching or what I actually wanted.

I started working on developing myself. Louise Hay's book: *You Can Heal Your Life* did just that for me. It helped me heal myself and my life.

At that point, I felt like I could do something to supplement my income. That observation of certain colours and clothes making me look and FEEL better piqued my interest more and more. I became obsessed with Trinny and Susannah and, in the end, I decided to train to find out what this colour analysis was all about.

Oh, wow! I was learning, I was studying, but I no longer felt drained, I was starting to feel ALIVE. I remember my boyfriend telling me that I had more energy for clothes shopping and my studying than anything else.

Subsequently, I set up a business as a Colour Consultant. I didn't really have a clue what I was doing when it came to actually getting clients, so I invited a group of family, friends and colleagues – twenty-two people in total – and put on a colour evening. I got four clients from that evening. My first PAYING clients. I was buzzing.

I repeated the evening and friends of friends came too. New clients were starting to trickle in.

When people had come and had a colour consultation (where I told them which colours look best on them), their next question was, "I know what colours to wear, but what style of jacket, trousers, tops should I wear?"

So, I went on to train to be a Personal Stylist. I learnt all about body shapes and why certain clothing styles and fabrics suit certain body shapes. It enthralled my scientific brain. I was hooked.

What I didn't expect was how much my health would improve as I started doing more of what I loved. It felt like I had a new lease of life. I was getting paid to do something that made me feel energised rather than the opposite. That all sounds great, doesn't it?

BUT...

Those insecurities started seeping back in. I knew I could dress up and look okay, but I still felt ugly. And I constantly found things to criticise myself about.

I ended up doing more things to hide behind the laptop and business dried up. I knew (deep down!) it was nothing to do with my skills but my belief in myself. It was all to do with my mindset!

I set about transforming the way I saw myself. I applied the principles I'd learnt to help me regain my health to regain my confidence. I knew I had to see my body and myself in a much kinder light if I were ever to succeed in business.

It worked.

I started putting myself forward to, and working with, large organisations, and collaborated with high-street stores, charities and even BBC radio.

The more I put myself out there, the more my following, exposure and client base grew.

I loved it but part of me felt sad that I was helping to style women who had felt like I had for so long – not good enough, not attractive enough. I became more and more frustrated that so many women were telling me the clothes and colours they'd love to wear but when it came down to it, they lacked the confidence.

"I'd love to wear that colour, but I'd stand out too much!" or "Do you really think I could pull that off? I'm not sure what others would think."

These weren't garish colours or in-your-face high fashion items. These were colours that looked amazing on them and styles and patterns they not only looked fantastic in but had told me they'd love the confidence to wear!

I knew at that point that I wanted to work with women on a different level. I wanted to help them with their confidence and body image.

I'd been following a top UK Coach for a while and when I saw that she was running Confidence Coaching training, I jumped at the chance. I'll never forget the day I walked into that Chelsea hotel and got to practise on my first coach-ee. I just KNEW that coaching was the thing I wanted to do. It felt so right. It's difficult to explain but when you know, you know.

I'm not going to pretend it was easy to transition and that I suddenly had a calendar full of coaching clients. It felt like starting all over again, in a way. But it was worth it.

As often happens, when the student's ready, the teacher appears; and I came across a very successful coach from the States who was running a year-long coaching program. What excited me the most was not so much the coaching part (I already felt confident doing that) but the fact it was also focusing on developing a business. I'd be learning how to set up the systems and structures of a business. I'd be learning from a multiple seven-figure female entrepreneur and I knew it was time to learn how to actually run a business rather than play the guessing game.

Not only did I meet some of my best friends during that year and had four amazing days in Paris at a conference (ooh la la), but I finally felt like a business owner. We worked on our mindset A LOT. Changing the way we saw success, money and bringing in clients.

I was able to put my business on the map, so to speak. I started working with clients across the globe. Plus, amazing new opportunities for joint ventures and features in international magazines came my way.

As wonderful as the publicity and success was, I can't tell you how incredible it was to see women transform in front of my eyes.

I had clients whose body-confidence was at an all-time low. One came to see me after her husband cheated on her. She felt 'ugly and unattractive'. In a matter of weeks, she stepped into her power and saw how attractive she actually is. She then went on to end the relationship and is happier in herself than she has ever been.

Another client was in her fifties and had been single for over twenty years. She couldn't see what she had to bring to a relationship. She learnt to see her beauty on the inside and out. As a result, she gained the confidence to sign up to an internet dating site, I helped her write a profile and, after a few weeks, she met the man of her dreams. They are now married!

Over time, I started attracting more and more women who wanted help with their confidence but were also business owners. So, once we'd increased their confidence, they asked me to help them with their businesses.

One of the first business owners I worked with was a massage therapist and, as a result of our coaching sessions, she went from five clients a week to twenty-eight a week and had to hire an assistant.

Again, I was hooked.

It was like all the pieces of the puzzle fitted together. Everything about my journey had come to that point and I had so much to share because I'd been running a business for seven years by then.

Whilst I still work with clients on increasing their confidence and getting clarity on exactly what they want to do in life, the majority of my clients are now female entrepreneurs.

I help them to have the confidence in who they are and what they do so they can put themselves out there in a much bigger way, grow their audience and sell their gifts. I also help them to set up the system and structures I wished I'd known about, and understood, all those years ago.

If you're reading this and feeling scared to take the leap to do something you love, I want you to know that everything you desire is not only possible but that you're 100% capable of making it happen.

You have to follow that dream of yours. I'm not saying you'll get ill like I did if you don't, but you'll always wonder 'what if'.

And I know you're not the woman to be happy with living a life of regrets.

If I can do this then so can you! There's nothing special about me. I finally listened to that voice inside and let myself go for it.

I full-heartedly believe that life is meant to be lived YOUR way! Oh, and best of all? You DON'T have to wait years (or even months) to start living your dream life! You simply have to take the first step.

I now not only LOVE what I do, feel so energised by it and feel blessed to call this my 'job', but I get paid more than I ever could have done as a teacher.

I hope my story helps you, the woman dreaming of MORE (whatever that more is for you), to know and believe that what you want is possible.

Listen to your gut and listen to those longings.

If you can dream it, you can create it. It's just about taking action towards making it happen and watch as life helps the magic unfold.

★ ★ ★

Emma Ward is a business confidence coach helping female entrepreneurs develop the mindset and business structures to get seen by their ideal clients and get paid to do what they love.

Emma is a teacher, entrepreneur, coach and speaker as well as the founder and creator of many online programs.

Emma lives in Berkshire with her partner, Matthew, and they're delighted to be expecting their first child in summer 2019.

She's obsessed with travel, spa days, Golden Retrievers, smoothies and working from cute coffee shops (with great Wi-Fi).

Connect with Emma and download her free resources at:
www.emma-ward.com/mof

9. Donna

Growing up in the 1980s, I was the typical overweight fat kid. I had a great circle of girlfriends, many of whom are still great friends to this day. I was always bright and bubbly, and made an effort to be everyone's friend. I was the "always there with extra cash for you at the canteen", and a "share my lunchbox snacks with you, in case you forgot your lunch" type of kid.

Looking back, I actually really enjoyed school. But each and every day felt like hard work, trying to put on a brave face, when deep down I was hurting. I was bullied about my weight on a daily basis. I couldn't talk to anyone about it. My sister and I are only thirteen months apart in age. She was gorgeous, tall and slim. I was short and fat. I loved her dearly but hated her guts at the same time.

I remember coming home from school one day, and I had had enough. I was exhausted, depressed, and I just couldn't do this anymore. So I opened up my wardrobe doors, placed my skipping rope around my neck, and looped it over the clothes bar. That was the day I tried to hang myself.

Turns out the distance from the bar to the floor wasn't long enough, so I had no room to dangle from the skipping rope. I guess I should have put more thought into my suicide attempt, as I clearly wasn't paying attention in maths class. I jumped on my bed, crying my eyes out, and reflected on my life. I had nothing to be upset about. I had fantastic parents, an awesome younger sister and great school friends (thank you Maree and Bree for getting me through my darkest times). I had no real reason to want to leave all that behind. Surely there had to be more to life, right? God must have put me on this planet for some reason. I just didn't know what it was, yet.

1996 was my final year of high school, time had flown by so fast, and I had no idea what I wanted to do with my life. My local hairdresser suggested I do my school work experience at her hairdressing salon. If I hated it, I was allowed to just sit out in the back staffroom and catch up on my homework, but at least I had somewhere to do it, to get my teachers off my back.

Wow! It was so much fun! I just loved chatting to all of the clients, seeing them all get their hair and makeup done for special occasions. I was taught how to shampoo hair at the basin, how to blow-dry hair, and I even started applying hair colour. I honestly didn't want to go home at the end of each day! My hairdresser filled out my work experience feedback forms for my school teacher, and she noted that my bubbly personality, enthusiasm and social nature were perfect to pursue a career in hairdressing. Hooray! I finally found something that I was good at, and I finally felt like I belonged somewhere.

The following year, I enrolled into beauty college and gained my first trade qualification in nail technology. Soon after, I started my hairdressing apprenticeship in a salon in Five Dock, which also offered acrylic nails services, so I got to do both hair and nails every day. It took two hours to travel into work, via two trains and a bus, and the same back home again. I was exhausted, and I missed out on going out to clubs on Friday and Saturday nights with my friends. I wasn't the stereotypical "blonde-haired bimbo" hairdresser, but I was good at it, and I loved making other people feel good about themselves.

By 2001, I had finally finished my hairdressing apprenticeship, and was happily working hard in various salons across Sydney, whilst my sister, Sarah, was working as a beauty therapist at the local beauty salon. We really enjoyed talking together about our work at the end of the day. our bosses were so mean, cheap and rude that we started brainstorming ideas in a scrapbook about our dream salon business.

After all, running a successful salon business runs in the family! My late grandfather owned and operated his own hairdressing salon in 1961, so continuing the hairdressing tradition in the family has been an honour, and I still keep all of his hairdressing tools and his old photos on display. My father and my aunties would spend their after-school hours and weekends at the salon with my grandfather.

I soon had met my ex-fiancé, Scott. He was tall and slim, and worked in travel and finance. A typical suit and tie kinda guy, and a total opposite to my ex Corey. We lived together for a few years and got engaged whilst on holiday in Bali. I remember he was down on bended-knee in front of everyone at the resort, they were all clapping and cheering, and all I could think about was praying for him to just stop and stand up. I was so embarrassed, and I quickly said "yes" to make it all stop! Walking back to the resort, I was dreading the thought of having to plan our wedding. I knew we had grown apart, and I didn't want to marry him. But we lived together, and that was the right thing to do, right? I mean, who else would love me?

In July 2004, my sister and I both applied for separate personal loans from the bank and found ourselves a local solicitor. We then went all in and purchased a run-down old salon in Croydon. It had been abandoned for over twelve months. With help from my dad, we spent two weeks renovating it, and opened up our first business in Croydon NSW. We were still driving two hours to and from work each day, but we loved it. We knew customer service, and we knew our jobs, but we had to learn how to run a business as we went along. Within the first six months, we had won our first local business award. That was a major surprise out of nowhere. To this day, we have no idea which customers had voted for us, or who our mystery shopper was. But that helped us stay on the right path, giving us confirmation that we were doing the right thing. Another six months later, and we had won both the NSW New Business of the Year award, and the Australian Most Innovative Salon in Marketing. We were self-taught, but we were clearly doing something right.

I loved my salon more than anything, and I preferred to stay back and work late most nights, rather than going home. Scott and I were very distant, and more like flatmates. We were at a stalemate. One of us had to have the guts to end it. So, one day, with the help of some clients, I just packed my car whilst Scott was at work and moved back home with my parents. I left my engagement ring on the bedside table. No note, no phone call. I knew he would understand and wouldn't contact me again.

I was back to being a workaholic with no friends. I never had any time to go out and meet anyone. I joined a dating website called RSVP where

I was "matched" with my now husband, Ryan. He had the same interests and hobbies and lived local. We had the same taste in music, and we both supported the same football team. He actually contacted me first, and, well, the rest is history. He was, and still is, perfect in every sense. Finally, life was bliss!

Like most businesses, we had our ups and downs. We had issues with landlords and rent increases, which saw us relocate the salon to Campbelltown in 2008, Eagle Vale in 2009, and finally to Smeaton Grange in 2010 where it remains today. The awards just kept rolling in, which would eventually see us win a total of ten awards and become a finalist in another twenty awards in just seven years.

One day, I kept dropping my scissors halfway through a haircut. I would drop the blow-dryer halfway through styling someone's hair. My knees would randomly give out, and the next thing I knew, I was trying to get up off the floor. Something was wrong, but no doctor could confirm anything. I remained on anti-depressants, and low dose anti-inflammatory medication to get me through each day. Due to my ill health, I had to sell my beloved salon to one of my employees in 2011. I was devastated, and I felt lost. I struggled to find a new job that I could settle into. So, I went back to study and added more hair and beauty qualifications to the list.

It was early 2008, and the time had come to buy my wedding dress, and therefore organising bridesmaid dresses. My mum asked me if I just wanted to ask my sister's best friends to be my bridesmaids, since I didn't have any friends of my own. WTF Mum? I know she meant well, but at that exact moment, I was heartbroken. I realised I was working my ass off, seven days a week, had a loving husband, but was wondering that there had to be more to life than just work.

The next five years saw us struggle to fall pregnant. By 2013, I was thirty-one and Ryan was thirty-five. I was petrified I had left my chances of becoming a mother too late. We were still workaholics who were constantly asked about when we were having our first child. The past five years of trying to conceive a healthy child, when we both had "unexplained infertility", were honestly my toughest years. Forget about the pain of being bullied as a kid in the playground, or the daily struggles of starting your own small business. Tring to conceive your first child, when you have unexplained infertility, feeling like your body was failing you, honestly had to be the most traumatic period of my life to date.

In June 2013, Ryan and I welcomed our first (and only) child into the world, Madison Rose. When Madison was just six weeks old, I woke up to chronic pain, literally everywhere! I couldn't even wiggle a toe without screaming in pain. I couldn't hold my baby, I couldn't breastfeed, I could hardly stand up to get to the toilet! It took three days to be able to have the strength to put on some clothes, get Madison in the car, and go see the doctor. They did a few tests and referred me to a Rheumatologist. I was thirty-two and diagnosed with Rheumatoid Arthritis. The Rheumatologist told me my pregnancy hormones were hiding the disease, and at the six-week mark, after I stopped breastfeeding and my hormones changed, I had the biggest flare of my life! He told me I would have a walking stick by the time I turned forty and be in a wheelchair by the time I turned fifty. I was devastated my body was failing me and depressed I couldn't be a normal mum and hold my baby like everyone else. I was now on daily medication for the rest of my life, and weekly low-dose chemotherapy drugs to help reduce the pain and inflammation, and to slow down the progression of the disease. There is no cure for RA. I had to put all of my new salon business plans on hold until I could sort out my health, whilst trying to care for a newborn baby.

I was told if I lost weight it would help to relieve the pressure on my joints, reducing the pain and inflammation, along with the added benefits of reducing obesity-related disease. So, after years of research, in January 2016, along with my husband, we both had weight loss surgery. I created a Facebook page to document our journey, and make myself accountable, in the hope of inspiring others to take control of their life and their health. Since then, my husband has lost 42kgs, and I have lost 50kgs – all of our excess weight. I have proudly gone from a size 24 to a size 10-12. With the weight loss came a new sense of self love. But it was hard to enjoy the results when I still had a body that looked like it was melting, with skin dripping off my bones.

September 2017 was the start of my plastic surgery journey. My first skin removal surgery was my arms and my breasts. I was back to work on the eighth day, and smashed out four days, only to pop some stitches open in my armpit, got an infection, and ended up with another week off work to recover. All went well, and I was booked in for my second skin removal surgery in April 2018, where I had a lower body lift with a fleur-de-lis tummy tuck. My confidence was growing, I had a new love for fashion, and I can now go into any shop I want to buy clothes. Unfortunately, there was still more to go!

In May 2018, I stumbled across my local MIBA networking group whilst scrolling through my Facebook newsfeed. It sounded really interesting, and the ticket price was low compared to all of the other local networking events in my area, so I purchased my ticket and was excited to go and meet some like-minded women in business. A few days before the event, I got a private message via Facebook from the event coordinator. She explained that the event had been cancelled, and that she had resigned from her position, effective immediately. She then asked if I would like to take over as the coordinator. Wow! Me. She asked me. I was super excited. Hooray! I had a new little side hustle that I could build and nurture. I had been operating several businesses, and had hundreds of business contacts, so I knew it wouldn't be hard to get my MIBA group and events up and running. The following month, I hosted my first MIBA Sydney South West networking event, and have done so every month, ever since.

I finally belonged in a tribe of women who are all there to support and inspire each other. I have reconnected with some old friends, and made a stack of new ones, whilst collaborating and building our businesses. Like-minded women who also understand the daily struggles of balancing a family, maintaining a home, running a business, and at times working a second job to ensure the money consistently comes in, in case business is slow.

In October 2018, I went back to hospital for my third skin removal surgery. I woke up from surgery and mention that I feel like I can't breathe. I felt minimal pain, as I was hooked up to all the meds. Instead, it felt like I was being squashed from both the front and the back of my chest simultaneously. I was on hourly observations, and all of the nurses' tests were normal, so I was discharged from hospital after two and a half days. I was sleeping most of the day away, and all through the night, only waking up when the pain relief tablets wore off, and it was time to take some more. The next few days were no improvement. I emailed my surgeon, who suggested I saw my GP immediately. I was sent off for an ECG, which came back fine, and then a CT scan, which I found very emotional. I cried the whole way through it. It showed I had collapsed lungs with fluid in the bottom of each. Oh great! I was back on antibiotics, and needed an extra two weeks off work. Holy moly! Four weeks off work, and away from my business. I was in constant pain and could hardly do anything. Even getting up to make a coffee was exhausting. A few beautiful women from my local MIBA tribe each contacted me offering to make me meals, or do my grocery shopping, or drive me to the doctor, etc. Wow! I couldn't believe it! I had several offers of help whilst I was housebound. I finally have friends who care! Honestly, I have been so humbled with the generosity of others. I am truly blessed.

There is so much to look forward to in the future! No doubt my life will be filled with family, friends and fun, whilst keeping fit and healthy! I hope to outsource some of my tasks, so I can spend more quality time with my family, and less time sweating the small stuff. I aim to make new connections through MIBA and collaborate with more women to build my tribe and grow my hair, beauty and health business. I am passionate about total body wellness, and supporting Australian Made and Certified Organic products wherever possible, which is why I joined Grace Cosmetics back in 2002.

I hope my story can be an inspiration to anyone else who is struggling with their weight, or suffers from chronic illness. Xx

★ ★ ★

Donna is thirty-eight, from Camden in NSW Australia, and is a proud mum to Madison, aged five, and devoted wife to Ryan. Donna is also the proud MIBA Networking Event Coordinator for Sydney South West, and owns a hair and beauty salon with over twenty-two years' experience. Donna has been a Grace Cosmetics Independent Distributor since 2002, and has won numerous local, state, national and international business awards since starting her first salon aged just twenty-three in 2004.

"I dedicate my chapter in this book to my daughter Madison Rose."
You are welcome to connect with Donna via any of the following:
Email: donna_sillett@bigpond.com
Website: http://www.macarthurmakeovers.com.au

10. Leanne

When I saw the opportunity to feature in this book, I just had to jump at it. For so long I have wanted to find a way to help anyone going through or living with any kind of mental health issues to give them a bit of hope. With so many people being affected by depression, anxiety and the rise in suicide numbers, if my story helps just one person, I will be so, so, so happy.

If you have never lived with someone who has mental health issues, it's quite hard to explain just how tough it is. You never quite know where you stand, things are going great then *bam,* it's all gone to pot again. It's exhausting keeping up with the highs and then getting through the lows. You don't understand why it is that when you give 110% love and support it's always you who gets the blame for any little thing that goes wrong. You start to walk on eggshells, not because you are scared, but because you don't want to make matters worse and you get used to being blamed for everything, you are almost waiting for it.

My husband went from love to hate very quickly and had no issue in telling everyone and anyone how awful I was and how much I ruined his life, only to then gain a bit of calm and clarity to later apologise and just carry on like nothing had happened. Then again something would happen outside of his control and I was hated and blamed again. It went on and on and on. When I look back now, I see clearly how strong a person I was in that moment as I took some pretty awful treatment, but my focus was always that he would get help, and all would be okay. It takes a lot of strength to overcome the feelings of someone you love, who calls you awful names, berates you, leaves you and the children for no apparent reason then comes back only to do it all over again, and again.

I didn't feel strong at the time.

I could see his pain, but I had no idea where to start to help him. So, I just stood by him. I kept a lot in about the whole situation, as people don't understand mental health. Any signs of someone being nasty to their spouse or having unpredictable behaviour and people instantly suggest you should leave them and not put up with it, and you are a bit of a mug if you don't. In fact, the whole time was a very lonely time for me, as dealing with it all meant I had to just focus on getting through and I couldn't keep up socially with friends or family. My husband was just different to other people's husbands. They couldn't relate. It was as if I had to stay focused because if I lost focus I would crumble.

I was also finding it very hard to stay on top of my own self-esteem and self-worth; having given birth twice within the space of eleven months, I felt every horrible word I was called like a knife to the heart. After childbirth, you kind of lose a little bit of yourself and your dignity in the readjustment period. Everything is wobbly, you are tired and fragile; I honestly could have done with a bit of moral support. But it was not to be. The stress and challenges on a day-to-day basis were just so draining and mentally exhausting. Wondering what mood he would come home from work in, worrying in case anything cropped up that would send him into a spiral.

We didn't have a normal relationship for such a long time, it was like going to war every day. His erratic behaviour spoiled so many special days, even our wedding day was spoilt. He refused to come to my mum's sixtieth birthday celebration meal because of some anxiety he had going on at the time; and I had to walk out of a family fundraiser because I could see that his thoughts were taking a bad direction and it would have all just ended in tears. I couldn't bear any more humiliation.

We didn't go out as a couple because he would excessively drink and just do ridiculous things, so I preferred to just stay at home. If we ever got invited anywhere, I used to panic about going and always make an excuse as to why we couldn't attend. He had absolutely no control over his own thinking, he would go off on a tangent and create twenty worst-case scenarios about what could happen and end up in a complete state of anxiety.

To cope with the anxiety he would try anything, drinking, drugs, excessive spending, obsessive behaviour – I was always sitting worrying, working out what bills needed paying. It was a huge weight on my shoulders. Huge. I felt the whole situation lived on my shoulders and I had to find the solution. It kept me awake most nights. When would he get help, would things ever change, how would I buy food, pay for the kids' clothes, buy nappies! I couldn't budget or plan financially because large amounts of money would just disappear from his wages, so I was always borrowing from Peter to pay Paul. I would lie awake at night working out which bills were a priority, what I could sell to cover them, how many days I had left before they were due.

I also spent so much time shielding the kids from it all, worrying if they had seen or heard anything. Wondering what I would do with four kids on my own if I did leave, how would I cope, how would they cope. My mind was just full, twenty-four hours a day, running scenarios over and over.

In an attempt to stay afloat, I set up a personalised craft business. I am forever grateful for this little business because, although I had to sit up sometimes until 3/4am in the morning painting Christmas Eve boxes for customers, this business was my sanctuary. I gained a bit of control back – I made money to pay the bills, I didn't have to lie awake at night worrying anymore, I could afford Christmas presents, I could afford food, I could put diesel in my car. That little business saved my sanity. I enjoyed so much interacting with my customers, coming up with new ideas and the boost I got when people actually bought things was massive. I even started to go to craft fayres and it gave me the boost I needed to get dressed, get my make-up on and make an effort to actually leave the house and put myself out there.

It was attending these fayres where I felt the most vulnerable and I saw just how much of a recluse I had become dealing with everything. Starting this business brought me back to life a bit, I felt good at something again. It was like a weight was lifted and I had a purpose and an escape from reality. Because the reality was pretty shit.

The day my husband had what they called a nervous breakdown was pretty surreal. I remember his behaviour and thinking 'My god, what on earth is going to happen?' He had totally checked out. He had no idea what was going on and was sitting staring out of the window saying over and over and over again how beautiful it was out there, as if he couldn't remember he had just said the very same thing two minutes earlier.

I remember feeling scared, I was on my own with two small babies living on a farm in the middle of nowhere. It took four phone calls before I even found someone willing to help, I was blown away. I remember trying not to cry, asking a receptionist at my local hospital, 'If he was having a heart attack I would ring 999, right? Who do you ring when someone is having a breakdown?'

Two more phone calls and eventually the crisis team agreed to come to the house and assess the situation. Three hours seemed like three days; I was trying to get my husband help, keep him calm, breastfeed one baby and keep the other baby occupied while my two eldest children were luckily at my parents' and thankfully missed the whole affair.

The crisis team were like two angels. They came in, calmed him down, promised him a consultant would see him the following day and all would be OK.

That night I didn't sleep a wink. Halfway through the night my husband had decided that the consultant couldn't help him and wanted to take his own life. He sat and told me, very matter of fact, what I had to do. I had to just get in the car with the babies and go to my mam's, then ring the police and not come back until they had removed his body. And he said I would be fine, and my life would be much better.

We got to the morning with me having spent hours trying to talk him out of it and listing all of the reasons it was the worst idea. He agreed to go to the local hospital for his appointment, but he was still hell-bent on taking his own life.

I honestly thought going to the psychiatric unit of a hospital to see a specialist consultant would be the light at the end of the tunnel.

It was the worst thing ever.

Long story short, he didn't help us. My husband got extremely agitated at the situation, so the consultant asked us to leave the building and to book an appointment with a GP. So, I was left alone with a suicidal husband, two infants and the light at the end of my tunnel had well and truly gone out. I remember saying over and over, 'But he has threatened to kill himself, I am by myself with two babies, what do I do if he attempts to take his own life?' The consultant said, 'Ring 999 and speak to your GP in the morning, I can't deal with your husband while he is agitated.'

Over the weeks following he saw several other doctors and was diagnosed with four different conditions, including bipolar, personality disorder and having had a complete psychotic break from reality. Each doctor had a different opinion, gave a different medication, but never a solution.

After a while, he began to calm down and come out of the other side. The talk of suicide stopped and he got back on track a little bit. It was the longest three-month period ever. Every single day I made him get in the car and I drove him all over; we went on adventures, days out, day trips – I was so determined to keep his mind occupied with the good stuff and didn't want him slipping back into feeling suicidal again.

Things were okay for a few months then again he went downhill, only this time he decided that it was better that he didn't live with me and the children because he was ruining our lives with his 'issues', so one night he packed and left. I remember sitting on my bed in total turmoil, on one hand I was devastated, but on the other I was relieved. Relieved to have a break from it all. I knew he would be back, and he did, of course, come back, but after such a crazy, stressful few months, in that moment he drove down the farm track, it was like a weight had been lifted. Like someone had taken the lid off a pressure cooker and all the steam was free to be released; that's exactly how I felt.

I felt so guilty for feeling this way because this man is my soulmate and absolute love, but I just felt so glad to sit in silence and just be. No drama, no name-calling, no worry, no eggshells, just silence. It was bliss.

I was so lucky at the time, I lived on an amazing farm surrounded by green fields and stunning scenery. It was like a retreat and I just sat that following morning in a gorgeous state of calm, looking out at the view. It felt like I could actually breathe for the first time in months. In that moment, I didn't know if he was coming back or not and I felt pretty bad about myself; I didn't like my appearance, I didn't feel good enough, I felt ugly, I felt worthless and unwanted.

I remember going to bed that night and praying to my grandma Margaret to help me get through whatever was about to happen because I felt like I needed a boost of her amazing strength.

The next day – I can't recall how I exactly came across Gabby Bernstein – but a webinar randomly appeared in my Facebook timeline and I watched it. And something clicked for me. Like a little spark inside of me had reignited and I was intrigued to learn more. I ordered the book on Amazon – *The Universe Has Your Back* – and I read it in one day. I then went on a study binge and signed up to every possible self-help concept out there. I was in such a bad place, but when I looked around and saw my four children all looking at me expecting me to be there for them, guide and support them, it snapped me into action.

I studied NLP, I got a bit obsessive and also signed up to learn CBT, EFT, mindfulness, life coaching certification, reiki – you name it, I just spent weeks absorbing all of this information. I felt stronger every day, more determined to get back to myself and also it felt like I could help my husband, as I now had the tools to do so.

I set up a Facebook group under the name of Mama Alchemist and invited people to join me in a little mindset challenge and I put all of the principles and techniques I had learned into practice helping others – this massively helped me to heal and the group of ladies who took part will forever stay in my heart.

A few weeks had passed since he had left, and I had completely turned my mindset around, reconnected with myself and I was so grateful for the journey that had brought me to that point because even in all of the madness I had managed to get to the eye of the storm and had found my calm.

Another few weeks after that and my husband had come back, only this time it was different – he had really had enough of his own shit and had decided to take drastic action. The light at the end of the tunnel did come, in the form of an amazing private rehabilitation centre in Spain called Step One Recovery. The centre changed his life and mine forever. In five short weeks they were able to bring my husband back to life. Not through talking therapies, not through traditional counselling, not through medication – but through love and understanding.

I remember when I went to pick him up from the airport, I was so nervous and didn't know what to expect, what to say or how to act. I was blown away; he looked ten years younger, the stress lines had gone, that awful pensive look he always had was gone, he looked fresh, happy and content.

I always used to say to him that I wished he could just get some peace in his mind and when he walked through security it was there – he had managed to get that peace.

This was over a year ago now and he has not had issues since.

Mental illness can break you if you do not have the right support in place, but it shouldn't be that way. It affects everyone around you, it takes its toll on them also, it's a journey the whole family take together, not just the person suffering. My husband has often said to me that if I hadn't stuck around, he doesn't know if he would be alive today or not.

I was so thankful and full of gratitude for the amazing people who took care of him at Step One. Now I am on my own personal quest to help combat the mental illness stigma and to get people talking about their emotions and to understand their thoughts and feelings. I completely ditched everything I had learned about mindset, NLP, CBT, mindfulness – it all went out of the window when I came across the three principles: the very same understanding my husband was introduced to during his stay in rehabilitation. It transforms lives overnight. Once you understand how you get to the point you do and how you are experiencing life day-to-day, it's like a lightbulb goes off in your head and all the drama and conflict and self-loathing just slides away. So, there is ALWAYS hope.

My mission is now to help as many mums, women and children to get to this stage of understanding of the human experience and just going out there, smashing it and having the best possible life!

My story ended well, and I have learned so much along the way.

It's pushed me into a career I was meant to have.

It's pushed me into letting go of everything that no longer serves me in life.

It's pushed me into just waking up each day and living my damn life.

It's pushed me into falling back in love with myself.

It's pushed me into not worrying about what anyone else thinks because I am doing just fine.

It was a journey I was meant to travel, and I am grateful for the lessons I get to take from it.

If you are living with someone who has mental illness, I send you so much love; hang on in there, get the right support, take care of yourself.

If you yourself are suffering from mental illness, you are not in this alone, you are loved, you are needed here, and you have so much to give – keep going.

★★★

Leanne is a mum of four and lives in rural Northumberland. As an emotional wellbeing mentor and founder of the Happy Mama Movement, she is an advocate for supporting mums and their children to live a happy and balanced life. Leanne started her career because she found herself at an all-time low and saw the impact her mindset had on her older children. She was inspired to educate herself and explore ways in which to maintain a better emotional balance in herself and her children and is now a certified mentor sharing the three principle understanding via her Mama & Me Positive Living Academy.

Website – www.mamaalchemist.co.uk

11. Debbie

Have you ever heard the phrase 'Watch out for the quiet ones?' Well, this is me in a nutshell!

I'm a workaholic! Yes, there you go, I said it. I live, breathe, sleep, eat (often to my detriment) events. But do you know what? I absolutely love what I do. It's my job to make people happy through the medium of events. This could be a wedding, corporate staff party or a themed experiential event.

It's the best feeling in the world knowing that I played a huge part in putting huge grins on people's faces.

Let me take you way back… I grew up in Berkshire. I was a shy kid with an afro, as my mum didn't know how to deal with curly hair. My parents had their own business, so it was usual for me to stay late at school most nights. We had lots of childminders over the years, who I remember for favouring my younger brother, as he was always the cute, funny, charming one. I was the quiet, fat kid.

At a young age, I went to work with my parents. I remember stuffing brochures into envelopes in my Dad's office or manning the phones on the reception desk. I really loved it as it made me feel really grown up.

At the age of ten, my mum took me to my first ever Weight Watchers group. I also remember going to a child psychologist regarding my weight and my mum was told I'd grow out of it. I went to boarding school for a few years, which I loved. Looking back, it probably gave me loads of independence too.

By the time I reached my final year of high school, I was a size 20, proper chubby! I always wanted to be liked by everyone and worried what people thought of me. I know there was some bullying going on, however

I didn't really let it bother me, I just saw it as immature behaviour and got on with life and worked hard. I wasn't top of the class in school, but I was a trier and I did well.

I had an entrepreneurial spirit from a young age and remember creating my very own hotel (made out of cardboard!). It was so organised. I had rooming lists, check-in, cleaning procedures and more! I always thought I wanted to be a hotel manager, but then realised I didn't fancy being stuck within the same walls every single day. I wanted variety, excitement and an opportunity to be creative.

When I was looking for a degree to choose from, I came across Event Management. The industry was much younger than it is now, and it wasn't the done thing. I read up on it and thought 'Yeah, I could do that, I can do business and events together. How cool would it be to have a career where you organise parties and events for a living!'

I've got very motivational and supportive parents who always pushed me to succeed. At the age of twenty-one, I went on a Dale Carnegie course; 'How to win Friends and Influence People'. This definitely helped me work through some of the 'quiet girl' barriers I had.

When I was growing up, my favourite time of the week was running my local Jewish youth club. Looking back, this is probably where my creativity stemmed from. We used to create some super fun educational programmes. I remember laughing hysterically at so many things. We were just a small group of kids who didn't care what anyone else thought, and it was all about encouraging and including everyone. It was a safe place. I was always encouraged and pushed out of my comfort zone. I abseiled, stood in front of 150 kids and leaders public speaking, went potholing and got stuck in a cave as my bum was too big! I was encouraged to use my creativity, dress up in stupid outfits, act and DJ on stage for a New Year's Eve party. I even led a street dance activity on the Jewish Sabbath (so that meant no music), which was probably a good thing since I am tone deaf and can't keep in time to save my life.

Following school, I took a gap year in Israel where I learnt a lot about myself. During this time, I asked my mum to send out my Weight Watchers books, so my friend Allie and I could use them together. We pretty much halved all our food we had, shared it and the weight dropped off. I made some lifelong friends. Even though I don't see them much now, I know we all have a special place for each other.

I went to university in Leeds to do a BA(Hons) in Event Management. In my second year, I did a placement with an event agency specialising in pharmaceutical events, working in the business development and events department. It was my favourite part of the degree. I know if I hadn't done this I definitely wouldn't be where I am today. I got to travel all over the world and stay in some luxurious hotels. My absolute favourite event was when I got to organise a fragrance launch for Procter & Gamble in Paris with brands such as Chanel, Hugo Boss and Lacoste. We travelled by Eurostar and my job was to personally chaperone a 3ft orange and white striped zebra prop under my arm! As you can imagine, I was trundling down the platform at Waterloo, zebra under one arm, and suitcases in the other, getting all sorts of strange looks. I had nightmares of decapitating the darn thing!

I lived in North-West London during this year and worked in Holland Park. In my hunt for a flat share, I remember going to meet two random guys in a Waitrose car park. It was pitch black, one was wearing a beanie hat and they both looked dodgy, but I followed them back to a random house to meet them. Luckily for me, I'm still alive and those two boys are two of my best friends today.

During my summers at university I had some great experiences. I did a season as a holiday rep in Faliraki, Rhodes. Foam party Fridays and bar crawls were the norm! I think it's the only time ever that you'd find me dancing on a podium in a club. I was completely out of my comfort zone but had the most amazing time. I felt like for one summer I was a completely different person. I was also top sales rep on the island, pretty proud of that!

The following summer I went to New York with a religious Jewish group, where I learnt loads about my Jewish identity and made some amazing friends.

I graduated from university with a first-class degree. It was like I'd found my calling, I knew what I wanted to do, and I was determined to be the very best I could be.

Before I had finished my final year, I had my first job lined up with the

UK's biggest Jewish charity. I got the job of event manager in London for the UJIA (this is the organisation who funded my youth groups as I was growing up). I was super lucky, it was a great first job. I got to manage a team of two. Knowing nothing about Jewish events, I Googled the names of some kosher caterers and when asked the question in my interview, 'So… Are you familiar with kosher caterers?' 'Oh yes, there's x and there's x,' I went on confidently. 'You seem to know them all, that's great,' said the interviewer. Thank goodness for Google!

I got to organise some great events; a dinner at the Grosvenor Park Lane with guest speaker Jerry Springer, a sports dinner at Lord's Cricket Ground, and a Major Gifts dinner at the Dorchester. Overall, the events I organised raised over £2.8million. I feel proud and privileged to have been part of these.

When it came to relationships, I had been dating a few randoms throughout university, I'd done the Jewish dating sites and had met some truly strange characters. I was like, 'Why are men such dicks?! All they want is one thing, and all I want is to find a husband and settle down!' It was not happening, I'd had enough, that's it, so I stopped driving myself mad, stopped looking, and gave up on men. I'd always been setting myself goals and remember telling my grandma Oma I wanted to be married by the age of twenty-five.

That summer, something special happened. I was living at the time with Martin, one of those scary guys from the Waitrose car park. Martin had grown up caravanning and camping and, as a tradition on the August bank holiday weekend, all the grown-up kids went camping too. So, it's no surprise that I got asked, 'Debbie do you fancy going camping for the weekend?' Martin and his cousin Ben encouraged me to go, so in true 'I don't travel light' style, I found the biggest tent I could find. It was seriously huge, with three separate pods to sleep in. Off we went to Stratford-upon-Avon for our camping weekend, laden down with everything but the kitchen sink. There was this guy playing the guitar at night and we started chatting. We exchanged numbers, from that day on we kept in touch and after a lot of texting we arranged our first date.

Our first date was an experience. Michael was from Manchester and I was from London, so we arranged to get together the next time he was down south. He came to pick me up and we headed off to West Hampstead. He was telling me how he found this gorgeous restaurant. So we got there and… the restaurant was completely boarded up. He said, 'I thought it was strange that nobody was answering my calls!' We had a giggle, it broke the ice, and we went to the restaurant across the road.

Career-wise I went on to work for an international management consultancy company, where I got to organise events all over Europe and South Africa for the most senior people within the world's largest organisations. This role taught me all about providing an excellent customer experience and this has stuck with me for life. I got to work with companies such as American Express, Cadbury, Unilever and HSBC. I even went to Nestlé head office in Geneva, which was amazing.

During this time, I had a phone call from a lighting technician I got talking to in Paris during my placement year asking if I wanted to go into business together. I always wanted to have my own business, so I thought, 'Why not?' We set up an event production company called Qube Productions. We specialised in staging and lighting for parties and corporate events. Paul had a load of his own equipment and I pretty much came on board and helped with the branding, admin, sales, etc. It was my first time in business, I didn't really know what I was doing. After a while, I knew things weren't right. Paul just wanted to spend money. I felt like I'd had shares in McDonalds with the number of receipts that went through the books.

Throughout this time, I continued dating Michael; lots of trips to Manchester every other week and lots of holidays together all over the world. Each time we went away I was thinking, 'Is this the trip he's going to propose?' I think I drove him mad with it. Finally, he popped the question on a holiday to Israel. We went to a restaurant overlooking the beautiful old city of Jerusalem from the David Citadel Hotel. He told me to close my eyes, placed the ring in between some sushi (my favourite food) and then popped the question.

The wedding planning began. I didn't do weddings at the time, so I'm sure it would be completely different if I were to do it now. The serious diet also began, firstly by cutting out chocolate for a whole year. I was obsessive about it. I remember eating a chocolate chip cookie and then spitting out the chocolate chips!

During that year we had to make the decision about where we were going to live. Michael didn't want to move to London, so I ended up moving to Manchester, which was really scary as I didn't know anyone. It was a new and exciting challenge moving to a city where nobody knew me and where I could make a new start. Now I love it.

Aged twenty-four, we got married. It was the most amazing day of my life. I'd lost loads of weight, the skinniest I'd ever been. Thinking back, I'd gone from a size 20 when I was at school to a size 10. I felt amazing.

I started remote working in Manchester and spent three days a week in London or travelling around the world, which I did until the financial crash in 2008 when my position became redundant.

The job hunting began. I remember ashamedly disguising myself walking into the job centre, thinking, 'What am I doing here?!' I was surrounded by all sorts of people, but nobody like me. There were no jobs that were remotely like anything I wanted or felt I was qualified to do.

One weekend, I saw a tiny ad no bigger than a matchbox in the local paper asking for help to plan a community-wide event, Salute to Israel, which was a parade and party in the park for Israel's sixtieth anniversary. I wrote a really long email to a lady called Joy Wolfe applying to event manage the whole event. I told her what she needed and asked her to let me help her. Guess what? I got the go-ahead! It did take over every moment of my life, but we organised an amazing community event attended by 6000 people. It was a great way of getting to know the Jewish community around me.

I finally got a job working for a law firm doing their marketing and events and, on the side, I continued with Qube Productions in the background. It wasn't going anywhere, so I ended the partnership with Paul and it was not long until I thought I could do this by myself, so I set up Qube Events & Productions.

About eighteen months later, I found out I was pregnant. I remember laying there with jelly on my belly all excited for our first scan, they found a heartbeat and moments later found another heartbeat, we were having twins! I don't know if my husband wanted to laugh or cry, it was a bit of a shock to us both and our parents!

One of the first events I picked up was randomly a vaginal surgery conference at the Manchester Science & Industry Museum – so bizarre to think this was one of my first events. I was still working at the law firm at the time. It worked out quite well as I could disguise meetings with my client at the hospital with pregnancy appointments.

I used to sneak into boardrooms to take client calls. No one seemed bothered, as I never let it affect my work and I always over-achieved in my day-to-day job.

All was going well with the pregnancy until we went for our next check-up scan. That's when the world came crashing down around us. There was only one heartbeat. I was devastated I'd lost one of my babies. It was the most horrible experience I have ever been through, I felt completely numb. I'd told so many people I was having twins, I had to deal with the consequences of telling people I had lost a baby. I carried both my children to thirty-eight weeks. It was a bittersweet day. I gave birth to a gorgeous baby girl, Dahlia, and a sleeping baby boy. We said our goodbyes to our baby boy and named him Doron which means a 'gift from God' and said hello to our beautiful baby girl Dahlia who has grown into an incredible strong young lady. We always wanted Dahlia to know about her twin brother. We often talk about him, we light a candle every Friday night and I always tell her if she is ever unhappy or feeling down to think of Doron as her guiding light who's going to help her get to where she wants to be. Dal, he's got your back!

I was determined to make my business work and properly launched it during my maternity leave. Michael basically told me that if I didn't make it work, I'm going back to work. I've never looked back since.

My father-in-law had an air-conditioning business that was based next door to a floristry shop and I used to spend lots of time in there chatting with an inspirational mother and daughter discussing options of how we could work together. I worked with them on a window display using mirror balls. At that time, a lady walked into the shop who got excited about the mirror balls; she was planning her sons Bar mitzvah. We started chatting and that's how I got my first ever party. I never planned to go down the party route, I supposed it just happened, but I've never looked back since. With this kind of work, it's all about word of mouth, especially in the Jewish market. The more I did, the more referrals I got off the back of it, and that's how the business grew.

I put on a lot of weight during pregnancy, proper ten-tonne Tessie! So, I decided to get myself a personal trainer and sort myself out. Every day I would go for a walk for an hour pushing the pram. I walked around the streets of Whitefield doing flyer drops.

It wasn't long before I needed extra help, so I took on a voluntary placement student who used to come to my house where I set up a mini office. We had one small wooden shelf of event props on a bookcase, which originated from my husband's bedroom as a child. Now that same bookcase is still being utilised and has become our spray-paint shelf lined with tins of different colours.

Through my events I came across a couple of brothers who owned a photography company. I was fairly new still in Manchester, so didn't really know too many people, however they took me under their wing and showed a huge interest in me and my business. They gave me lots of great advice and support and introduced me to some great contacts.

As years moved on, we shared office space together and we also became an arm of their business. There were no official ties, we just promoted each other to clients and both generated a lot of work for each other. I learnt loads, which I am super grateful for. As time passed, we both spent a lot of time in each other's businesses and it started to become draining for us both, so we went our own separate ways. I knew I was the expert in my field and I needed to go with my gut and do what I do best.

So, I was on my own, and it's probably the best decision I ever made. I found my wings and I could fly! Nothing was going to stop me.

I opened up an event studio with my team of three at the time. Now we are fourteen strong! I took a huge stand at the National Wedding Show and went all out. This really took my business to a new level, but it was petrifying. I remember I didn't sleep the night before our first show, fearing our stand would fall down or that nobody would show any interest. In reality, we had an unbelievable response. Everyone loved what we did, and we booked some huge weddings off the back of the show. The organisers were so impressed with us that we are now in our fifth year of being the Official Venue Stylists of the National Wedding Show.

We quickly found ourselves winning contracts off some of the top florists in Manchester. I think this is where I started to believe in myself.

I know I looked far too much for help from others, whereas actually, if I just got on with it, I could achieve great things myself.

In 2003, I entered The Wedding Industry Awards thinking how amazing it would be to gain recognition for what we do. I didn't think we would have any chances of winning. Well, I was wrong again! We came away with Best Wedding Planner in the North West, 2013 & 2014. As we progressed into the décor and floristry market, we then entered the venue styling category and became National Winners 2016 and 2017. I couldn't believe it. That little business I started at home is now the best in the UK! Every year this gave me more and more of a boost to succeed. We had to live up to this reputation, constantly pushing our team to new creative levels. In 2018, and again this year, I was given the honour of judging the awards, something I am immensely proud of. We also won Best Creative company in Bury.

I love building new connections, so I reached out to a company in London about becoming their North-West décor partner. As an off shoot of this, I started investing in décor items to hire out and also launched the hire side of my business, Qube Event Hire. The aim was to grow to be the North-West's largest décor supplier. Now we supply décor to venues, venue stylists, wedding and event planners, event agencies, corporate companies and more. As time went on, our stock just grew and grew. We've invested in dancefloors, lighting, thousands of luxury silk flowers and also bought our very own floristry studio in-house.

The business just kept growing. Year on year we doubled our turnover, at the same time I was running around trying to bring up two gorgeous girls; I'm still running! I spend as much time as possible with them, but do I have mummy guilt? Absolutely yes! I have an amazing close bond with my kids, but I constantly feel like I'm not a good enough mother or that people think badly of me for not spending enough time with my kids. My husband Michael is so supportive. I taught him how to make Friday night dinner and, now he doesn't work on a Friday, he's taken over this role in the house. I never in a million years thought that this would happen, but it has, and I have learnt to accept it.

My job is all about making people happy and helping make amazing memories. However, I need to remember how important it is to make my own memories, cherish that time with my kids and my family, and make it special.

As my company is constantly growing, it naturally comes with new challenges. I'm learning new things every single day and jumping over hurdles along the way, which is making us stronger and stronger. I'm at the fortunate stage where enquiries are coming in so fast, we are putting systems in place to deal with them all. We're working with some huge international companies and organising some super luxe parties, including the Queen Charlotte's ball. I'm loving the variety and loving the challenges of growing the business. It's not easy, some days it's super hard and I think why am I doing this, however there is a light at the end of the tunnel.

Often people pay most attention to those with the loudest voice and most to say. However, I'm definitely an 'introvert'. Society often pays most attention to those who make the most noise, and this is a mistake. It's a misconception that some people think that quiet people are weak and lack intelligence. I suppose I still worry, am I good enough? I'm super grateful for the opportunities people have given me and for the future opportunities that I've not experienced yet.

I've learnt you've got to have a 'can do' attitude, work hard, and if you put your mind to something, you'll do well at it however many challenges life throws at you. If something gets you down, pick yourself up, and keep going. Surround yourself with positive people, believe in yourself and believe you're bigger than you are, and you'll grow into those shoes. I know I'm not great in huge crowds and I'm quiet, but that's OK. For those who take the time to get to know me on a one-to-one level it has enabled me to build amazing connections and we've achieved great things together. I've now got a reputation for being unflappable, super calm, with tonnes of patience and for having a super-active creative mind.

If anyone ever tells you that you're not good enough, prove them wrong!

I've got fire and excitement in my belly to achieve more and do better, as I know the sky's the limit and there is no end to what I, or in fact YOU, can achieve.

Believe in yourself and sparkle.

11. Debbie

★ ★ ★

Debbie is owner of Creative Event Décor planning and hire company, Qube Events & Productions, Qube Event Hire & Hollywood Letters. Debbie runs a team of fourteen and loves planning and styling creative events for companies, organisations and private individuals. Debbie has a passion for turning dreams into reality through designing and planning creative events. She is also passionate about helping others succeed in achieving their dreams.

Debbie is a multi-award-winning Event Stylist & Event Planner. Debbie is thirty-seven years old, mum of two gorgeous girls, Dahlia, age nine and Sophia, age six, and wife to music teacher Michael.

You can contact Debbie at:
www.qubeevents.co.uk

Follow Debbie on Facebook and Instagram @DebbieMarks

12. Jo

From the outset, my childhood was idyllic. We had very little money, but still went on holiday every year, mostly camping or caravanning. There was a lot of love in the house, my lovely nan and grandad were always around. We lived in a smallish village with woods and fields surrounding us, that was our playground, and we would disappear for hours and just come home for dinner.

Looking back, it's difficult to pinpoint exactly when my mum started drinking. My dad worked away a lot, sometimes for weeks, mostly for months at a time. My mum would take herself off to bed frequently with a 'migraine', she gradually became more and more sad and her bedtimes got earlier and earlier. We never saw her drunk, but it was obvious that she wasn't coping. As the eldest, I would cook and clean the house and make sure we all had clean uniforms for school. Then dad would be home, and everything returned to normal.

At the age of nineteen, my world suddenly changed. My lovely and beautiful aunt died suddenly, aged thirty-six, of a brain aneurysm. My cousins were only seven and ten, they had no mum, and their dad was grieving and very lost. They lived in Sharjah, in the UAE, where my uncle worked for an English construction company. I was studying to be a teacher (early years) in Canterbury, Kent, UK, about to embark on my final year. My uncle asked if I could go help out while the boys were on their summer holidays, as a paid nanny. I didn't even know where the UAE was – I had to go to a library to look it up in an atlas! I looked after the boys for the summer, and fell in love with a British guy, who worked for my uncle. He was twenty years older than me at thirty-nine years old, but we just really hit it off. It got serious very quickly. I knew I wanted to be with him, but was worried about other people's opinion around the huge age difference. I soon realised that the only opinions that really mattered were my parents. After a few months, we went back to the UK together for a couple of weeks. My parents met him and were incredibly supportive. We flew back to Dubai overjoyed and committed to each other. It seemed I was there to stay!

I immediately got a job in Dubai (fifteen minutes away) at a special needs school in Jumeirah, right on the beach. I was delighted to be in charge of the nursery class. It was wonderful, I had just six children in my class – all with severe disabilities, ranging from hydrocephalus to cerebral palsy, and most were local children. It was incredibly hard work physically and emotionally. The other staff were a mixture of Brits, Irish, Danes and Emirati. I carried on my studies via The Open University. This was way back in 1984 (YES! I am that old). Believe it or not, Dubai was a tiny city, surrounded by beach and desert – not one skyscraper. It was heaven. We had a boat, I took up waterskiing and windsurfing, we went camping on deserted beaches most weekends… (sigh!) I knew that I was here to stay for a while, and that this was a great place to bring up a family.

I had Sam aged twenty-four. It was a difficult pregnancy, I started bleeding at four months (unaware that I was pregnant, I had been clifftop diving), and had to have six weeks of bedrest. There was a lovely lady that I knew, a Filipino lady called Cora, who had been a carer for one of the local children in my class. Unfortunately, she had been really badly treated (abused) by her employers. We became friends, and when I became pregnant, she left her job and went back to the Philippines. When Sam was four months old, I went back to work and Cora returned to look after him. It sounds crazy – he was so little, but we only worked from 8am to 1pm. It was great for all of us. I then had Anya, and by then I was working at a local nursery school – and Anya just came to work with me.

By this time, we were very aware that Mum had a drinking problem. It all came to a head when my dad had to go to Nigeria for five months. My brother and sister were really worried about Mum, she was drinking heavily, not eating, the house was in chaos. I quit my job and came back to the UK with the children, trying to be there for Mum and stop her drinking. It seemed to work. I stayed until Dad came home, then went back to my home in Sharjah.

We moved to Oman when the children were still young. I worked for an International School there. Then I managed the nursery school for The British Council for a while. I also taught ESL to Omani and French children and adults while there. Oman is, quite simply, just beautiful. We had a fantastic lifestyle, we were at the beach or pool most days after school. I carried on diving, we camped, explored… everything was great.

Then my life hit a huge bump in the road…

I moved back to the UK, after seventeen years abroad, because of divorce. My marriage had been limping on for years and we had grown apart. After a while, I met Paul; Sam, Anya and I moved in with him and his two daughters and became a 'blended family'.

The following years were tumultuous. I lost my ninety-three-year-old nan to neglect in a London hospital, she had gone in quite well (a ninety-three year old who looked about seventy and was fearsomely on the ball and extremely intelligent and independent), but had an infected bunion that needed to be treated. We thought she would be in there for a day or two at most. Unknown to us, she picked up an untreatable infection. She spiralled downhill and after forty-eight hours was delirious and dehydrated. The staff outright lied to us about her condition; other patients on the ward told us that she had fallen out of bed one night and had been left, crying and distressed, for several hours before being lifted back to bed. I arrived the next day (we lived miles away and I was working and had four children to look after at home) to find her unresponsive. She had aged twenty years in forty-eight hours. She died four days later. It was a horrific experience for us all.

Shortly after this, we lost my beautiful, kind younger sister to suicide. Anyone who has been touched by suicide will know the shock and agony that this brings. It was devastating, absolutely devastating. In the following years there were always questions and guilt. "What could I have done to help her?" "Why didn't I see?" "Why didn't she tell me?" "Why couldn't I save her?" These questions followed me for years.

Just a few years after this, my dad died in horrible circumstances, after a short and vicious illness. My dad was the kindest, loveliest man; to watch him suffer, and not be able to help him, really haunted me. His last hours were nothing short of horrific. I was on my own with him; my mum was in the hospice too, but was in a state of shock. I stayed with him, talking to him, trying to comfort him, until the end.

After this, my mum just sank, she gave up. We had a horrendous year where she was slowly killing herself. We were so desperate to help her, fight for her and get her well. She came to live with us for a while, and she would put on weight and stop drinking. Then she would demand to go back home – and it would all start again. I had to put her into rehab twice – but, despite everything, she just went down a path of despair/alcohol/refusal to eat. She didn't want to live, it was a slow suicide. Towards the end she was hospitalised, weighing just five stone. She died shortly afterwards.

This was all in the space of six years.

I had become Deputy Head teacher for a pupil referral unit (PRU). Most of the pupils were 'looked after' children, living in children's homes; it was tough to say the least. Every day consisted of verbal and physical abuse on the staff by these 'lost' children. They had been let down by parents/family/society and had so much anger and hurt. We provided education and therapy, but it was very much an uphill struggle and it took a toll. I had also remarried, with all the stresses and strains of having two families merging. My confidence and self-esteem were rock bottom, and I was drinking too much. I was sad, angry, frightened, guilty… I knew I had to do something because I was heading for self-destruct. I was diagnosed with bipolar type II. I was struggling big time!

So – I got therapy, lots of it and different types. I also moved back to early years teaching – and it was this that became a solace and a joy.

I could see that so much of our curriculum in the UK is centred around academic achievement. Hardly anything on emotional well-being. I started to see how child and adolescent mental health services (CAMHS) were struggling to see children we deemed worthy of attention. I saw parents struggling with their children's behaviour and emotions. I had witnessed, first hand, what mental illness, stress and anxiety can lead to. How it can destroy lives.

I was on a mission – a mission to help teach parents how to foster emotional well-being and resilience skills in their children. I'm a good teacher, I just am. I'm also one of those people who (annoyingly for some) kids just LOVE. I wanted to share what I know.

My husband backed me all the way. We started our own company, 'Tiny Sponges', and I left work. I wrote some books around activities to do with early years children, which I thought would be my first product. I also wrote a Christmas book for children, I started a blog and my blogs started getting published. I was prolific in my writing and output and was also learning a lot about the intricacies of social media and business. But I hadn't got to the 'publishing/earning anything' stage. My husband was extraordinarily patient – and he believed in me. He saw me. That was my blessing.

I, by now, had two social media groups for early years parents. One around learning and development, the other around helping parents teach emotional well-being and resilience skills. I also belonged to various parent groups. One thing that came up often last year was the impact of blanket media coverage on young children. Mainly with terrorist events, there were A LOT, and every time something happened parents would be asking, "What has my child seen or heard?" "What do I tell my child?" "Should I say anything?" "What should I say?" Parents themselves were anxious: "I don't want to take my family to London." "I'm scared of being at an event with my family." I looked for advice for parents and found very little. No books. Especially not for younger children. BBC Newsround had a great video, but it was aimed at nine to fifteen-year-olds. Then Grenfell Tower happened. Same remarks from parents: "I'm worried/my child is scared…" In a day I had written the bulk of my book. I knew it would help people and I knew that I was the right person to write it. It became my mission.

Why was I the right person to write this book? Great question! Well, I lived through the IRA bombings, and had two close calls. I missed one bombing by a day – another by an hour. I lived through a military coup in the Middle East, through a difficult time in the Middle East, when there were wars, invasions and hostage-taking – which included two of our friends. I witnessed a horrific and fatal house fire in my small village when I was very young. My son was exactly the same age as Jamie Bulger. I KNOW that parents and children worry and get anxious – but I also know that talking about things, knowing what to do, and having a plan eases that worry and anxiety. I've been there. I have several T-shirts. When the zombie apocalypse comes, you'll want to be on my team!

So, my husband and I make a bloody fantastic team! I am the creative – and he is EVERTHING else! We had self-published the book. It was illustrated, edited, all ready for launch and promotion. Then I became very ill.

I didn't know what was happening to me to be honest. I thought I might be going mad. I was getting flashbacks of my sister's suicide, my dad's death – when I was awake! They were so vivid. At one point I was awake for three days in a row, too afraid to sleep because of the nightmares I was having. I was emotional, angry, sad, frightened… I lost all my confidence and my self-esteem was rock bottom. I couldn't vocalise what I was experiencing, just couldn't get the words out because I was scared to death.

Eventually, my husband dragged me to the GP, I was then referred to a psychiatrist, and within ten minutes had been diagnosed with Post Traumatic Shock Disorder. It was a painful journey to recovery, through EMDR (Eye Movement Desensitisation Reprogramming) therapy – but I made it. I continued to work – and we launched my book at Waterstones with a reading and signing. I have just published my second book, and we have had so many business opportunities come our way. From being a shivering wreck, who didn't have her photo taken for twelve years, I'm now able to face going out, talk to people, to do live videos.

One of the main turning points for me was becoming coordinator for MIBA West Sussex, Brighton and Hove. The support and friendship I've found through the group has been life enhancing. I manage the group online and arrange and coordinate the meetings. It has definitely taken me out of my comfort zone, and has fostered a new confidence in myself. I am even speaking at conferences now, to people I've never met before. It still scares me a little, but I'm on it. My self-esteem is back.

Life is good. It throws you some curve balls – and you never know what's around the corner. But life is a big, bloody miracle – and it's up to us to learn, adapt, power through, help each other and contribute. It's also the only life we have – so do it in style, do it with love, do it with integrity, but just bloomin' do it!

★ ★ ★

Jo is coordinator for MIBA West Sussex and Brighton. She is a teacher and parenting advisor. She also runs 'Tiny Sponges' social media groups for parents, with a focus on helping children's wellbeing, robust mental health and resilience skills.

Jo is a published author and blogger, she has written two children's story books *How To keep Safe… in a sometimes scary world* and *Cold Toes at Christmas*.

Jo Fitzgerald lives on the south coast of England, with her husband and dogs.

www.jofitzgerald.com

13. Melissa

From the outside looking in, a lot of people might think that I have it all, and that it was easy to get to where I am now. I have a beautiful family. I'm in the top 1% of my Network Marketing company. My family has the time freedom that we want. And yet, things aren't always what they seem from the outside.

This is a story about how I went down a spiral of self-doubt and mental illness and still came out with a success story to share.

My deepest desire is to bring awareness to the people who don't understand what mental illness truly is, and to bring hope to the people who have been suffering in silence.

This is my story.

I can't claim that postpartum depression totally changed me. Because, let's be honest, I was dealing with mental illness before I had my first daughter. I was first diagnosed with depression in college (since then I have been diagnosed with ADD and anxiety as well). But when I became pregnant for the first time, things got a lot worse. I was anxious all the time. I would obsess over everything because it was the unknown. I felt so out-of-control about it all. It still embarrasses me to admit this, but I would draw floor plans of how to arrange our bedroom. I would draw the crib next to our bed, and then would draw where I would sit on my bed to feed my child. I felt like I had to map everything out because I didn't know how to be a mom. I was so afraid I would do it all wrong.

I became obsessed with attachment parenting books because I felt this uncontrollable need to make sure I wasn't damaging my child. I still believe in the principles of attachment parenting, which are breastfeeding, co-sleeping, baby-wearing. The theory is to provide your baby with a secure attachment so they feel confident when they get older. In theory, it is amazing, but in reality, for me, it might have made things worse. Any time I would put Avery down, I would get an overwhelming fear that she would think I abandoned her. Here she was, a tiny baby, and I kept thinking that she would feel terrified that she was abandoned or that I somehow didn't love her if I just put her down to do the dishes. Now, it didn't mean I didn't put her down, but I was carrying that anxiety and that guilt with me when I did EVERYTHING. And I couldn't understand how some moms were able to shower and do their hair and put on make-up. I honestly remember wondering, 'What do they do with their baby while they do these things?' I was living in an irrational, scary world and I had no control over it. Or even any real knowledge of how bad it was, despite my husband trying to tell me. And I was overwhelmed. Oh, I was so overwhelmed. And tired. So very tired. I would feel like a failure every single day.

I was a mess; our house was a mess. And I was a stay-at-home mom, so it made no sense why our house was a mess (or so I thought). I get it now, there aren't many stay-at-home moms with spotless houses, but at the time, to me, it meant I was a failure. I was so used to being good at what I did for work. No matter what line of work I was in, I somehow always was promoted, or winning awards. But as a mom, in my head I was a failure and it was just pushing me farther and farther down a rabbit hole of despair.

Things started to get a little better for me the older and more mobile Avery got. As I started to get the hang of it, I began to feel a little of my anxiety release. But I still didn't realise how much pain I was in, and I certainly didn't express any of it to anyone. Not my husband, not my friends and not my family. I was literally suffering in silence. Part of me didn't even realise that what I was experiencing wasn't "normal", and part of me suspected it wasn't, but I was ashamed to admit how I felt. If you had asked me at the time, I would have said that I was just anxious because I was sleep deprived.

Just before the birth of my second daughter, Emma, I confidently told my husband that things were going to be different. I was convinced that I had some sort of control over what happened to me before. But the minute Emma was born, I realised I was 100% wrong.

It's true, I had more confidence in handling a newborn, but I also had to figure out how to parent a two-year old and a newborn. The fear of failing both of them overpowered me. The days were filled with not knowing what to do with both girls, keeping up with the house, cooking and getting Avery to classes. The house was the first thing to go. I justified the absolute chaos going on in my mind by saying I was not a housewife, but a stay-at-home mom. I thought that if I focused on my kids, that was what was most important. But, in reality, I couldn't keep up with a thing. I couldn't be consistent with any system I tried to set up. I was falling deeper and deeper into despair.

Finally, I decided to talk to a psychiatrist. It had been a long three years of suffering, and it took this doctor all of forty-five minutes to hear what was going on in my head. I was irritable, angry, frustrated and consumed with guilt and obsessive thoughts. He told me I had postpartum depression and he suspected I had it with Avery as well. I told him I wasn't depressed. I wasn't sleeping all day, which is what I thought depression was. And he told me that's only because I can't go to bed with two little kids needing me. He also said I should be proud because he knew I worked hard to take care of them as well as I did. Some mothers who suffer with PPD are not so lucky.

There is no way to express the hell I was living in my head during this time. And even if you had the most supportive spouse or family or friends, no one can fully understand PPD unless you have experienced it. It's scary, lonely and chaotic, and all while trying to care for an infant. When I'm around people who see a baby and say they have baby fever, I cringe. I actually cringe at the thought of infants. I love my children with all of my heart and I would do it over and over again to have them. But I, unfortunately, wasn't that mom who was able to relax and be easy going. And the worst part is I wanted to experience that, and I felt a tremendous amount of shame that I couldn't.

Once I started taking the medication I was prescribed, I started to get into a groove. One day, I remember scrolling Facebook and seeing many of my friends joining network marketing companies and finding myself longing for something more. My friends looked happy. My husband and I were both stressed at home, I felt isolated and alone. And I still felt like a failure as a mom because I still had unrealistic expectations of what a stay-at-home mom's life was like. I felt like I had to have everything together, and it wasn't happening for us. I'm not sure why, in the midst of coming out of a postpartum depression, still feeling overwhelmed and isolated, I thought it would be a good time to start a business, but I did.

I saw an ad for a new company in a niche that had never been done before in network marketing, hair care. The products were naturally based, which is important to me. I had a gut feeling that this could be a huge opportunity if I worked my butt off in the launch of the new company. When I first joined, I was excited. But throughout it all, I was also terrified. It brought up all of my self-doubt and fear of judgment.

But I wanted to make this work for my family. I wanted the financial and time freedom that I knew was possible in this industry. I had a gut feeling that this could be a huge opportunity.

So, I went "all in". What went from a little "side gig" became an obsession to get our family out of the stress we were feeling. I knew network marketing was a vehicle to have the life we wanted for our family. And I knew I had a chance to make it work. So, to work I went. I had an inexplicable burst of energy as I started to navigate building my company online. But I had no real idea of what I was doing. And I didn't want to reach out to my friends and family in person. So, I decided I wanted to build this all online, approaching strangers on the internet. I didn't want to have to go to networking meetings or leave my house. So, I figured I would figure it out. I had energy that I hadn't felt in a long time. For the first time in a long time, I was in a community of adults that encouraged each other, and I was trying to learn as much as I could about this business. We were a new company, so there was really nothing set in place yet. We were kind of the blind leading the blind. But a couple of months into it, I found my groove in taking what I knew about in-person networking and relating that to online. I began forming relationships, and meeting people through Facebook. And people began to join me in the business. I was winning incentive trips, and reaching ranks that would secure profit-sharing for my family.

I found it hard at first to balance working with my family. I felt this need to reach a rank by a certain time and I was justifying working on my phone all the time. I didn't know what I was doing, so I was very inefficient. I felt responsible for my team and prospecting for new members and I became consumed with it. It became an issue in my marriage that I was committing so much time to my work, when I didn't have time or energy to get our house in order. I needed to find balance, I needed to make this work. I was desperate to have a life that I knew this opportunity could provide.

Flash forward one year and a half.

So, there I was, a top leader in my company, I had a team of thousands, my husband was able to sell his chiropractic office and we moved to Atlanta to be closer to family. We had all the time freedom we could want. You would think I would be happy. And I thought I was. But I was battling an internal pain that I didn't know how to regulate. I was seeing both a therapist and a neurofeedback doctor. And, once again, from the outside looking in, people probably had no idea I was suffering. I was making friends at my kids' new school, playing with my girls, working my business, and trying to get settled in a new city. But I was irritable, snippy, and my husband and I were struggling to connect. At one point, my husband asked me if I would be interested in looking into a program he had found online. It was for an outpatient program at a mental health clinic. At first, I thought, 'Really, why would I need to go there?' (I guess my anxiety and depression were harder to hide around my family than around friends). Then I looked at the description. The program was from 10am-4pm every day. It offered classes like mindfulness, yoga, meditation, art, understanding depression, anger management, overcoming anxiety, understanding your values, self-esteem class, to name a few. At first it was hard to say yes because I still felt so much pressure to keep my business going, and to be just as involved with my daughters. The thought of releasing that control felt scary, but also a relief. I agreed to go. We told our daughters that mommy was going to "summer camp".

Being admitted to an outpatient program played massive games on my mind. It was an interesting experience, one I will never forget and forever be grateful for. On the one hand, I felt such a sense of ease and flow and grace there. My anxiety melted away. I had a structure, and took classes I was interested in. And, ironically, I was still building my business when I was there. I could message with team members and sell shampoo on my lunch breaks from my phone. So, I guess you really can fit network marketing into the nooks and crannies of whatever you are doing.

But, even though I felt at ease, I started to wonder if something was really wrong with me, something worse than "just depression" or "just anxiety". I had a full psych test done and, while waiting for the report, I started making up other diagnoses. Week after week, no matter how many examples I gave them of why there was something "really wrong" with me (I mean, maybe I was manic and that is why I had so much energy when I started working?) they told me those were my distortions and that is part of my depression. I thought I had something "worse" than depression because I still didn't understand what depression was. I told them that I wasn't sleeping all day and crying, that I was running a business and taking care of a family. But I came to understand that depression has as much to do with how your negative thoughts take hold of your mind as it does with being "down" or sad. In a way, you live in an altered reality, you see things in a distorted, negative way. In my program, I learned to "check my facts". What I was thinking might not be as close to reality as I thought it was.

For example, during this time, I would all of a sudden feel like a failure and a fraud. I felt like I didn't even know the right shampoo to recommend, even though I had over one hundred happy VIP customers that I had helped in the past. Thank God for my sponsor for being so supportive. I clearly remember sitting in the lobby of "summer camp" and having all of these people reaching out to me to buy my products. And I felt frozen and stuck, like I would suggest the wrong product. But my sponsor was there to reassure me. And this is where mental illness is so crazy. I did know what I was doing, I had been doing it for two years at this point. And it is, in fact, not hard to recommend the right products. But I had told myself that I didn't know what I was doing. And that is how the spiral starts.

110

Every class in that outpatient program was fascinating and I ate it all up. This wasn't couple's counselling, which I had gone to before. This wasn't me talking to my therapist about the struggles with my kids or my marriage. This was 100% focusing on the care I needed to fully understand what I was dealing with, and how to make my life better. And it was hard work. I didn't take it lightly.

I remember sitting in a class on depression where people were talking about the stigma of it. Only three of the people in the group were open with friends and family that they struggled. I remember being horrified, ashamed and thinking I wouldn't tell anyone I was in there. I was embarrassed. I thought people would judge me. I carried that shame around the whole time I was in there. Even though, when I told the few friends I did, their reaction was one of "I wish I could go to summer camp". Or "That sounds like a place I need".

Every week I would go to see my counsellor and she would ask the same depression questions. And I remember one week when she told me she thought I was in remission. Remission! That is like cancer. That is serious. I had been there for a couple of months and at that moment I had an even greater understanding of how serious mental illness is. I was surrounded by people suffering from anything from addiction to personality disorders to postpartum depression. I could see how painful all these conditions were.

Towards the end of "summer camp", I realised I was healing. In every class we had to say what we were feeling. This in itself was difficult for me. I actually realised that I didn't have a good grasp on what I was ever feeling. I would answer "fine" and I was told that isn't a feeling. Learning to name my feelings, as elementary as that sounds, was a big part of my healing. Anger, sadness, joy, contentment, frustration. I had to relearn what I was even feeling. Because I certainly was not "fine". And, eventually, I felt a light go on inside of me. I felt brighter, I felt focused, and I felt happy. You don't really hear too many people use the word "happy" in those environments, but that is when I knew my time was coming to an end there.

Once I was out, I had to acclimate to getting back to my life. I was ready, and I had tools that I could use to help when I felt dysregulated. I had a much more thorough understanding of mindfulness practice and self-care. Before, I had always felt guilty or would say that I didn't have time for self-care. Now I know it is imperative for my mental health. I came away with binders of information on how to effectively communicate, which I still struggle with, or how to validate, or what my values are. The experience was utterly priceless. And there is no way I would EVER have been able to do this for me and my family if I wasn't in network marketing. If I didn't have the time and financial freedom to take four months to go get the help I so desperately needed. I am forever grateful for this industry and the impact it has had on my life.

Shortly after I finished the program, I was sitting in my car on mental health awareness day. I saw a funny meme about mental health that someone posted. I wanted to post it as well, but was afraid it would imply I suffered from mental illness. I didn't want people to think I was weak, or damaged, or not good at my job. I still felt that after spending four months in my program. But, this time, I pushed through the feeling and I posted it anyway.

A couple of days later, a woman reached out to me on Facebook. She wanted to know if she could talk to me about me being her sponsor. On our call, I quickly discovered that she was in another company and they had a team of people who wanted to add my business to theirs. The initial thoughts that bounced into my head were the usual ones: "Well, she won't choose me." (This is how automatic our negative voices can be.) But, at the end of the call, she said, "I want to join your team."

She told me that she had been following my posts and I seemed authentic and real. She saw my posts about mental illness. So, all this time, I was afraid of being myself, with being okay with who I am. All this time, I was afraid it would turn people off and so I had to portray perfection on social media. That I was a "boss babe, building her empire". When, in reality, I WAS a boss babe building an empire on social media, even if I didn't feel like it. And most importantly, people want real. All of us struggle with some type of insecurities. All of us have fears and fear of judgments, no matter how perfect our lives look on social media.

Do you want to know the secret of building a successful business? Be okay in your own skin. Don't apologise for who you are, because you will attract the right people who need to be in your life. They say your vibe attracts your tribe. If that is true, which I have found it to be, then I will attract a whole lot of women who might be suffering with mental illness, or have insecurities. And I am okay with walking this journey with them. Because my greatest passion is helping people realise their true potential. Helping people realise it is okay, in fact it is imperative that they can be unapologetically themselves. Every one of us is unique. And we need to stop beating ourselves up for being who we are and wishing we were something else. I am done feeling guilty for being a hot mess. I embrace it. I am not good at planning or organising things, but I have other amazing gifts and talents. What are you done feeling guilty about? Because it is time to release that guilt and grow into your greatness.

Through this journey, I gained a real understanding of what mental illness really is. There is a stigma, and people who experience it carry an immense amount of shame. Part of you feels like it is something you can control, and that you should be able to snap out of it. But you can't. It is a real illness and a real disease. Like any disease, you can't just will it to go away. But unlike cancer or a broken leg, there is nothing physical that people can see. And the shame is so strong that it's hard to let others know what's going on inside your head. Unfortunately, many people don't get the support that they would receive if they had a different kind of illness. By sharing my story, my hope was to expose what it feels like to suffer, and how it is possible to get help.

★ ★ ★

Melissa Swaney lives in Atlanta with her husband, Shane, and two children, Avery and Emma. She is passionate about normalising network marketing and mental illness. She is in the top 1% of her company and looks forward to helping women truly understand that they are enough, just the way they are.

She can be reached using the following info:
Website: www.melissaswaney.com

14. Michelle B

My journey to becoming an entrepreneur was not really an easy one. Although most of my cousins would believe that I was born with a silver spoon in my mouth, I had to work just as hard as anyone else to get where I wanted to be. I was born in 1971 in Hackney, London. My parents came over from St.Vincent in the West Indies in the 1960s. I have fond memories of my school days. I was a popular child, even though I was and still am an only child. Friends were always knocking on the door for me to play out. When me and my mum used to go walking down the street, all you could hear was, 'Watcha!' Back then, that was how we all greeted each other.

My parents always wanted the best for me and tried to make sure that they gave me whatever they could. I still remember my very first piano lesson at the age of five; little did I know that this would continue for the next ten years, until the age of fifteen (on achieving grade five) when my piano teacher died.

I went to the local primary school, which was across the road from our house in Stratford, East London, and I attended there until I reached the end of year five, when I was ten. My mum was never really happy with state education and was determined to send me to a private school. She was a midwife at the local hospital and actually delivered some of my friends' siblings. After school each day, I would go to the childminder's house. I don't remember my mum ever picking me up from school. I don't remember it bothering me, though. But one day she decided that she wanted more out of life, more time to spend with me. So, she decided to become a primary school teacher. She trained while I was in primary school. I was really proud of my mum. My dad worked at Ford's car motor company in Dagenham. He used to do two weeks' days and two weeks' nights. Every day, on his return from work, he'd bring me a Yorkie bar. I loved it when my dad took me into work and showed me the cars and where he sprayed them. I was very proud of my dad and I think he was proud of me.

In 1982, I started attending the John Loughborough school in Tottenham, North London. Back then it was a private school. I remember my mum writing the school fees cheques whenever they were due. I loved my days there as I really got to know myself and my cultural identity. I was celebrated for my achievements on a regular basis. In 1988 I was one of the first to sit the new GCSE exam. Unfortunately, I didn't get the expected grades in all of my subjects and had to enrol at the local college. At college, I worked hard and the following year got the grades I needed to start studying for A levels. I chose French and English language studies at A level and also took Spanish at GCSE level. In July 1990, after only one year studying Spanish, I got an A! I couldn't believe it!

That year, on my birthday, approximately ten friends and I went out to celebrate. It was my nineteenth. We had planned to go to the Oasis nightclub in Dalston, but it was closed, so we went to Trendz nightclub in Stoke Newington instead. It was packed! This guy pulled my friend for a dance. They looked really awkward together. Afterwards she complained that he couldn't dance. A few tunes later, when the lovers came on, I felt someone pinch my arm. I turned round and shook my head to say 'no'. But this guy wasn't taking no for an answer. He pulled me to dance. He danced offbeat and I found it difficult to move to the same beat. We danced the rest of the night away. Later I realised that it was the same guy that my friend had danced with. This became a running joke for years to come as he was the man that I would later marry.

I finished my A levels in the summer, and then went off to university to study languages. I remember sitting in the lecture theatre one day as the French lecturer was cracking jokes and I couldn't understand a thing he was saying. I hated the course and I hated living away from home. After a term, I decided it wasn't for me. My parents tried to persuade me to stay there, but I was unhappy. I dropped out. I got the silent treatment from my mum and dad for a while. They didn't want me at home doing nothing. I applied to do a BEd in primary teaching at Southbank university and I got in! It was a four-year degree, each year consisting of a teaching practice.

At first everything was perfect! I was doing well on the course and loved going into schools. I made lots of friends at university and enjoyed the social life. I'm still in touch with some of them today. I travelled daily to Southbank from Ilford to Elephant and Castle. Towards the end of the summer term, when I was almost at the end of my second year, I found out I was pregnant. I couldn't believe it. I couldn't tell my parents about it, as they were so strict. It was difficult to hide it as I was feeling sick all the time. Being in school on placement didn't help either, as there were so many strange smells. My senses were heightened. Although I hadn't mentioned it to my mum, she knew I was pregnant because she had been dreaming of fish. She would ask, 'Michelle, are you pregnant?' I didn't admit that I was until I really had to. When I finally told them, they were so upset and annoyed. I had the silent treatment for a while. I used to come home and stay in my room to avoid the atmosphere.

My pregnancy was a stressful one, worrying about my course, where we were going to live, how we were going to survive, since I was a full-time student and not receiving a grant.

On 5th November 1994, I went shopping with my mum down to Ilford. We were getting ingredients to bake a cake, since my mum's birthday is on the 7th November. I had been feeling uncomfortable that day, but didn't think anything of it. When we got back home, I was feeling tired. I decided to have a bath. I noticed a kind of mucus but again didn't think anything of it. As I got in the bath, I felt my stomach drop. It was quite a sharp twinge. I had my bath and got out. I started to experience cramping and back pain. I went in my room and bent over the bed. The pain wouldn't go away. I felt like I needed to go to the toilet. So that's what I decided to do. But nothing! I was now in so much pain. My mum and dad were planning to go out for my mum's birthday. I went downstairs and told my mum. She immediately touched my stomach and said, 'You're in labour!' I had another twelve weeks to go yet! We phoned the hospital to let them know and my parents drove me straight there. I was still wearing my pyjamas. On arriving, I was examined by a midwife and told that I was fully dilated. Within thirty minutes, Arron was born. There were so many staff. He was extubated, connected to tubes and put straight in an incubator and taken to the special care baby unit. That night was so weird. I was given a side room on a ward with lots of happy mothers. All I could hear were babies crying. But I didn't have my baby. He was a little fighter and was off the ventilator in under two weeks. But, one day, when Arron was just two weeks old, I went to the dentist to have my wisdom tooth extracted. I had a call from the hospital. Something was wrong, and I needed to come to the hospital. When I got there the doctor told me that they suspected that he had meningitis. They said he was seriously ill. The doctors didn't think he was going to make it through the night and told us that we could baptise him. Arron did make it through the night and many nights after that. When he was six weeks old, I brought him home. It was such a strange feeling, as there were no machines to warn me when he had stopped breathing. I had arranged with the university to take a few weeks off and then continue with the course, but because of his early arrival, I had to take the year out.

The following year

As arranged, I restarted the new academic year again, but found it very difficult getting to school placements on time because I had to rely on his dad, who lived in Hackney, to come and look after him. In the end, I decided to just complete the degree without the qualified teacher status. I bonded with a new bunch of colleagues and motivated myself to get back on track. I returned to university to complete the final year of my degree. Everything was going smoothly and according to plan until I fell pregnant again. I was devastated. Not only had I lost my baby weight, but I was geared up to complete my course as an early years primary teacher. The pregnancy didn't run smoothly. I was in and out of hospital due to suspected premature labour again. I went in at twenty-three weeks and again at twenty-seven weeks and had to stay for several nights whilst they gave me steroids to mature the baby's lungs and steroids to stop the labour. But luckily, this time my daughter, Rhianna, was born at thirty-nine weeks, only five days early. I remember the doctor saying, 'Congratulations Miss Blake, you made it!"

At this time, all I had left to complete my degree was my 10,000-word dissertation and my final exhibition. The university gave me an extension until December. It was such a fantastic feeling when I had completed it. But I was disappointed that I had given up my qualified teacher status.

After graduating, I looked for jobs, but decided that I really wanted to teach, so I went to do a PGCE in primary teaching, which lasted a year. It was tough! Lots of late nights doing assignments, and different teaching placements. Luckily, my parents were very supportive. Arron stayed with them during the week and came home at weekends and Rhianna went to a private nursery. I qualified as a primary teacher in July 1999. In the early days, I devoted a lot of my time to my work. I loved teaching. I loved being able to give something back to the community. In 2000, my partner at that time proposed, and the following year we were married. At first, married life was good, but we soon experienced difficulties and, in 2008, we separated. By 2014 we were divorced. During the time of my divorce application, I met my partner Bee. He was everything that I had hoped for. Being with him made me realise how much I had missed out on. I hadn't even been to Nandos until I met him! We got on so well, being just three years apart in age. His life was tough too, as he was caring for his mum who had dementia and his dad who was blind. Even though his life was so demanding, he still found time to fit me into his busy schedule. After being together for two years, we moved in together. In March the following year, we bought a home together, which is where we are living now. In April, Bee proposed. My little ray of sunshine, Myla, my granddaughter was born in September that year. Once I met her, she brought a new meaning to life.

2018

It is now 2018, I have been teaching for nineteen years. During this time, I worked hard to climb through the ranks in teaching, holding various positions such as year group leader, art leader and a phase leader. One day my partner said I'm not a risk taker. This made me think… I wasn't! I always played it safe. I decided to apply for a position as an Assistant

Headteacher and I got it! I did this role for three years. But this wasn't enough for me, I still wasn't happy.

I was introduced to network marketing through a cold market add. The products were lovely. But everyone I spoke to thought they were expensive. I didn't do very well with this company and I'll tell you why later.

My upline heard about this fantastic opportunity to start a ground-floor company and invited me to join with her. At first, it was all hush hush and I had to convince friends and family to come on board with me. Some did, including my mum and daughter. I was juggling the business and teaching full time. I managed because I wanted it to be a success. Just before Christmas, Bee's mum died from dementia and we had to fly to Jamaica to bury her. When I came back to work, the atmosphere was different, quite frosty. It wasn't a happy place to be. I found myself sinking into a deep, dark hole. I remember driving to work one day in tears. The drive to work was approximately forty minutes. I cried all the way to work, dried my tears, walked into the building, said good morning then went and sat in my office. I felt so depressed. Inside I felt like I could just get up, pack away my things and go home. But I didn't. This went on for two weeks. Little did I know that Friday would be my last time in that school. When the weekend came, I couldn't sleep because I was anxious about going to work. When Sunday night came, I was awake all night. At 5:45am on Monday, I tearfully got out of bed in a state because I knew I couldn't go into work, having not slept. So, I called in sick.

The next day, I went to see the doctor. He did a test, then declared that I was suffering with moderately severe depression. He then put me on antidepressants. It was the first time that I had spoken to anyone about how I had been feeling and it was a relief. I spent time investing in me. I read self-development books and listened to inspirational CDs and began my weight loss journey. My mindset shifted back to a positive one and, for the first time in a long while, I actually believed that I could achieve anything. I set to work on my goals. I updated my vision board, joined various networks and did courses to help me to be better at my business. During this time, I received a letter from occupational health. My school had requested that I attend an appointment. The doctor was very supportive and understood how the stressful environment had influenced the way that I was feeling. A few weeks later I then had to attend a meeting with the head of school and someone from HR. They didn't even ask me how I was! I sat there thinking, 'These are the people that I work for and they don't really care about my health!'

Five months on, I have left that school and I am in a better place. I still have the odd down day, but I am doing what makes me happy. I'm building my business (okay, I am involved in a few different businesses). I hit two leadership promotions in June and I'm now even more focused on becoming even more successful in helping my team achieve and fulfil further goals. My goal is to be able to work on my fortune, building my business. I'm not there yet, as I still need the income from my job, but one thing I do know is that I don't want to return to a life of stress. My well-being is too important. The reason why it didn't work out for me in the previous network marketing business was because I didn't have a strong 'why'. This time I know that my 'why' is strong enough, because it has pulled me out of the dark!

I am still in the teaching profession, teaching full time. I'm running my businesses part-time around my job and I'm beginning to love life again. When I wake up each day, I show my gratitude for everything that I have before working on myself. Investing in me is the best thing that I learned to do this year because it has enabled me to tackle anything and maintain my positive mindset.

Why?

My aim is to have time freedom to be able to do what I want to do, when I want to do it. I want to be able to take Myla to school and collect her from school whenever I can. I want to never have to struggle for anything ever again in life. I want to be able to retire from teaching by the age of fifty. I want Bee and I to be able to travel to different places around the world.

★ ★ ★

Michelle, mum of two and nanny to one, is currently working as a full-time teacher, whilst managing her business. She lives in Chislehurst,

Bromley in Kent with her partner Bee and her daughter Rhianna. You can find out more about Michelle here: https://www.facebook.com/MLB44/

15. Tara

Not all inspirational stories have to begin with a sad beginning. In fact, mine was exactly the opposite of that. I had a great childhood and come from a beautiful, loving family. I am truly one of the lucky ones. Sure, we have our ups and downs, but it's the journey together as a complete unit that moulded me to be the person I am today. I didn't need to look too far for inspiration or for someone to look up to. I come from a family with lots of inspirational people and my absolute idol will always be my mother. I am the eldest of four children, but we lost a sister who gained her wings too early. The loss of a daughter and the loss of a sister fractures a family in that very instant and, although all of those little breaks and splinters can never be put exactly back together, you learn to live with the cracks and learn to accept those little tiny holes where there shouldn't be any at all. Through all her grief, my mother still never faltered. She kept going on those days the darkness wouldn't leave her and truly lived her life to take care of us. Through all of that darkness and all of the heartbreak my mother carried us through and worked tirelessly and still does to this day to support us all. She ran her own business, became a director and co-founded a product line, and still never wavered, even when the youngest of my siblings was diagnosed with cancer last year. My mum didn't crumble, she didn't show that she was afraid she was going to lose a second child, she kept her sanity and once again found that strength and carried us all through that darkness that thankfully had the brightest light at the end of the tunnel. So, as you can see, I have a lot to live up to and can only hope that my children will one day look at me with the same admiration.

15. Tara

I am blessed with my life. I met my husband Andy and fell in love fast and hard, it was a sweep you off your feet kind of love. We got engaged and then married four years later, and we were so lucky to fall pregnant quickly and without trouble. Everything was a dream, and everything was perfect. We were hopeful and blissfully naïve about perfect births with birthing pools, gas and air, natural births and completely wrapped up in a dreamland. We attended the neonatal classes, and everything was going to be a breeze. The thing is, no one ever tells you about horrendous births and births that can go wrong. No one tells you the gory details about how your baby could get stuck because your pelvis is twisted, how I nearly lost my life, how we nearly lost our daughter and my husband nearly lost his sanity. I also didn't even know you could haemorrhage from giving birth and that could go through full reconstruction. Thankfully, Indie was born healthy and, after being stitched to high heaven, I too recovered well. The time came for all three of us to be discharged from hospital and start our new journey together. I will never forget that feeling of putting that baby in the back of your car after leaving the hospital. Andy drove so slowly, and we looked at each other with absolute fear. "What do we do now?" It was the most bizarre feeling. Suddenly we had a baby, our baby and we were as excited as we were scared by how much we had to learn. How we would have to learn to be parents but also as equally how we would have to adapt to the changes in our relationship too.

Not long after we had Indie, we moved to a gorgeous house in a new area. I was working part-time, but quickly fell pregnant with my second. I had always wanted two children, but you see I hadn't planned to fall pregnant so quickly. In an ideal world we wanted to fall pregnant with our second child when our first child would be entitled to free childcare so that I could keep working, but of course life doesn't always work out the way you thought it would. I started to panic about how we would cope financially when I should have been elated and excited like I was with my first pregnancy. I already felt that I had failed my child. I was plagued with all these doubts and this made me feel like the most ungrateful, horrible person and I didn't deserve this truly amazing gift growing inside of me. I knew people that were struggling to conceive and here I was thinking about the damn timing? What on earth was wrong with me? Little did I know that those little doubts would one day come back to haunt me.

My part-time wage didn't cover the childcare costs for two children under two, so I had to give up my job. We welcomed my gorgeous boy Tate into the word via C-section and, for me, due to complications from the birth of my daughter, this birth was a million times better than the first. Of course, the recovery comes with a completely new set of rules, but he came, he was healthy, and life was perfect. It's funny, though, for those people that think that a C-section is the easy way out and that you are somehow not as worthy to be a mother as those that have pushed a baby out, let me tell you something, I've done both. Neither one is easy and neither one makes you a better mother. At first, everything was wonderful; we were excited to be starting yet another chapter as a family of four. Indie was excited about being a big sister and again everything was blissful, perfect and full of new beginnings. When Tate was six weeks old, he developed bronchiolitis. Seeing your baby so poorly and struggling to breathe was one of the most terrifying experiences in my life. As a mother, all you want is to keep your babies safe, so no harm comes to them, but unfortunately life isn't like that. Tate got better and stronger and with the relief came, all of a sudden, a big black cloud that started to surround me. I don't know if it was the fright of seeing Tate poorly and wanting to keep him safe and cocooned at home, or if it was me that didn't want to venture out of the house as I felt safer at home or if it was just easier to stay at home with two very young children. See, no one ever tells you just how lonely motherhood can be and how all of a sudden you're not 'you' any more, you're not the confident business woman you know yourself to be, you're sitting at home with two babies with no one to talk to and you have to learn a completely new you... the mummy you, the housewife you, the jobless you and the lonely, anxious and no confidence you, and it's scary. And then the guilt sets in... you're guilty for missing your career, you're guilty for your life not to be enough, you're guilty for not earning money, you look on social media and then you feel guilty that other mums are coping so much better than you and their lives seem so perfect with their homemade Play-Doh, the homemade sensory toys, the homemade vegan casseroles, teaching their toddlers French whilst you are struggling just to keep the house in order, struggling to find time and even the energy to try and take a shower, trying to prise the toothbrush from your toddler's nose (French, indeed?!) and make sure both kids are scratch free, and have eaten something more nutritious than Wotsits and are still alive at the end of the day. The problem with today is that women are put under so much pressure. To be the perfect wife, the perfect mother, but this social media picture-perfect lifestyle is not real. People do not post the pictures of the kids screaming because you took the disinfectant away that they want to drink. They don't post pictures of themselves and their houses when they are dirty. Instead we get the good parts, and usually on a day you're feeling shit about yourself, just to make you feel worse.

So, my maternity leave was going to end shortly, and money started to run tight. We knew that we couldn't cover the childcare costs and it was then that my husband suggested I set up a beauty salon at home. It would be perfect. We could work around the children and each other's schedules. Sounds perfect, right? Unfortunately, with the months of loneliness and isolation and lack of socialisation came the lack of confidence and I really didn't think I could start a business. Especially not knowing anyone. Who would even come? How would I start a client base?

The doubts started to set in and every day I would talk myself out of the idea. Eventually, we had no choice but to go for it. Also, my husband saw my trepidation and bought my couch, trolleys and furniture for me and cleared the spare room, so I couldn't back out now, could I? For weeks I went between the feeling of excitement and the feeling of terror. Excitement from choosing the best products to stock, choosing the treatments I would offer and decorating the room all pretty, however those feelings of self-doubt always crept in. Would it work? Would people come? I remember reading a quote online by Erin Hanson which has stayed with me in the forefront of my mind and it was, "What if I fall? Oh, but darling, what if you fly," and honest to God that gave me the strength to at least try and believe in myself. Well, the day came for my first opening day and I already had clients booked! I couldn't believe it, and with each day I got more and more. With the help of social media and word of mouth my business started to take hold and from there it started to flourish.

Six months after starting the business, Tate became unwell. He went to bed the previous evening perfect and smiling but woke in the morning with a fever and very docile. I phoned the doctor for an emergency appointment and was seen almost immediately. The doctor told me that he had an ear and throat infection. I questioned this as he had seemed completely normal the day before. He wasn't off his food, he wasn't pulling at his ears and he wasn't whinging at all. As a mother, you know your baby, and I really didn't think he had this right. However, I was told that's what it was and that he would "get worse before he got better". And with that I was dismissed, being made to feel I was an overreactive parent that didn't know what they were on about. As soon as we stepped through the front door to our home, Tate was physically sick and then started to roll his eyes and go floppy. I immediately called the doctor back and told him he definitely has this wrong, this is different, I was petrified. He told me to take him straight to the hospital. I drove straight there, constantly looking behind me and checking him in his car seat. All of a sudden, I saw his tiny body lull forward and go floppy like a little rag doll. It wasn't like he had just fallen asleep, it was like he had just 'gone'. In that instant I screamed this bloodcurdling scream to try and wake him… I thought my baby boy had literally just died in the back seat. In that very instant, I was pleading for God to take me and just keep my baby safe. The drive to the hospital felt like an hour rather than the five minutes, I honestly hardly remember that drive at all, it's as if someone or something took over my body to get us where we needed to be. All I remember is running to the children's ward carrying his limp body in my arms and screaming at someone, anyone, to help us. Tate was taken out of my arms and placed on a bed, he was poked and prodded, wires seemed to wrap around his body like a thousand snakes. They checked his ears and his throat, it was then confirmed he didn't have an infection in either of those places. I knew I was right and, in that moment, I couldn't have hated a person any more than I did that doctor that saw us that morning.

After checking Tate for all the normal places of infection, I was then told that they were going to start treating him for meningitis. That word. That scary, harrowing word. It's a single word that can shake you to your very core, pull you into a deep abyss whilst feeling like you are in a massive room filled with nothing. I can't even put into words how I felt when they said that word; I don't know if I screamed, if I collapsed, if I cried. All I remember is a nurse holding me very tightly. I was blaming myself constantly that I'd somehow caused this, that those thoughts of doubt when I was pregnant with him were to blame. That God was punishing me for being so ungrateful for the gift that he had given me and now he was going to take him away. I prayed so hard for forgiveness and for him to punish me and not my baby boy.

The hospital started treatment almost immediately. It wasn't until three hours after Tate was hooked up to an intravenous drip that he started to develop a rash. It wasn't the typical rash with little red dots either, he was just purple. The doctors said that I acted very quickly and in most cases the rash is one of the later stages. They congratulated me in trusting my instincts as, if I had listened to that doctor to just expect his condition to get worse before it got better, he would have been far worse off or even not here at all.

Tate thankfully recovered very well and, after a week of hospital treatment, he was allowed home. When you go through a situation such as this, nothing else matters. Nothing. Not the perfect mothers making you feel inadequate on social media, not the cleanest house, not the best designer clothes for your children. Nothing matters anymore. All that matters is that your family is safe, loved and healthy. You look at the world in a different light. You appreciate the little things more and realise how very lucky you truly are.

With Tate back to good health and the business going from strength to strength, I too became stronger, more empowered, more confident, and my self-worth started to increase also. I know there is no greater self-worth than your babies relying on you and you providing them with love, nourishment and support, but this was something else. I was doing this for them, of course, but I was also doing this for me.

My clients will never know that, although they come to me for treatment, to feel listened to, to feel beautiful, it was actually each and every one of them that helped me every day. I see so much strength in so many people. It makes me realise that everyone has their own struggles and you are not alone. I am honoured to be a part of these amazing women's journeys through lives, to laugh with them in their good times and to hold them when they are going through the bad. They continue to help me achieve my goals as, without them, I wouldn't be where I am today.

For me, my work isn't a job, I love doing what I do. To be able to change those insecurities a person has, to make them feel more confident, to give them a little bit of time out from a very stressful world, or even to just talk to and listen to them talk about their own lives makes all the difference. They say that if you do a job you love, you will never work a day in your life, and this is so true for me.

To any mother going through what I felt, I want you to know that it's okay to feel upset. It's okay to feel scared. It's okay to feel overwhelmed. It's even okay to feel angry, but most importantly it's okay to be not okay. Remember that EVERY mother has shit days too, every toddler will throw a tantrum, every house gets messy, what you see on social media are the good days and the good moments and, trust me, you'll have thousands of those good moments and they will always outweigh the bad. You are the most important and the most adored person in your baby's life. You're doing amazing, trust me. x

★ ★ ★

Tara is a wife to Andy, a mummy to Indie and Tate and a beauty therapist/ skin specialist to many at Beauty Box Bromham. Based in Bedfordshire, Beauty Box Bromham offers many award-winning specialist treatments and aesthetics. *Mumpreneur On Fire 4* is her debut as a co-author. You can contact her below:

https://m.facebook.com/beautyboxbromham/

★ ★ ★

Tara would like to dedicate this chapter to her beloved sister Charlotte, for the life you didn't live will always live on in mine. Your memory is our greatest treasure.

16. Stacie J

I was born in 1984 in Blackpool Victoria Hospital. I lived in a council flat, in a small town called Fleetwood, with my mum, dad and sister for about nine months. We then moved to a council house, as the flat didn't have central heating and was cold and damp back then, so I was told by my mother in later years. We stayed there for around two years, then moved literally around the corner and this is where my memories really began. I don't remember anything at this point as it was 1986 and so I would have been around two. The earliest memory I have is my mum and dad's wedding, as I was a bridesmaid, and I remember the lady down the road who made my dress; we kept visiting her for alterations (this is a fond memory, as the lady was a lovely and gentle woman), but this is vague as I was still very young; it was in 1988, so I would have been about four and a half! I can't remember that much of my parents' wedding day.

Although I do remember they argued quite a bit after that day. This was because my dad started taking drugs and inviting friends round for a smoke and a drink and isolating my mum; her role was just mother and housewife. Then, as my dad's habits escalated, things turned worse, and that's when the domestic violence started! They say drugs change people and they certainly changed my dad back then as apparently, so I'm told, he went from being a loving, kind, caring man, whom had been in a bit of trouble with the police when he was younger, to becoming an evil, controlling and violent person. He would go out drinking and come back and start on my mum then start hitting her. I remember him hitting me and my sister once as we had been sent to our room for misbehaving and then he said, "One more word out of you both and I mean it," and us, being kids, tried to push our limits and made one more noise, and that was it, he came upstairs and smacked our bums, and God did it hurt! I also remember him battering my brother and smashing up his favourite video of Bruce Lee, snapping it over the bottom of the banister in half! Another vivid memory I have of living with my dad was when he and Mum were arguing. We were sitting in the living room with Mum, she was on the armchair and either myself and my brother or sister were on the arms of the chair. She'd not long had her fourth child, my brother, I think he was about five months old, so he would have been in his crib in the room with us, I guess, and I remember him charging in and dragging my mum out of the chair by her hair and beating her up. That was a scary moment as a child.

Later that night, he had his friends round and we were all in bed, including my mum, and I remember her waking us all up one by one and gathering us all together by the front door and getting my little brother in his pram and creeping out of the front door and running to my nan's, which was about two streets away. My mum had had enough and left my dad that night, but when he realised we had gone he came round to my nan's house. I was asleep, but woke up to all this commotion and remember looking out of the bedroom window and seeing my dad skipping down the alley laughing and making funny noises like a psycho, like he had gotten a kick out of what he had just done. When I went downstairs, I could hear my mum and nan crying and I think my sister was too. When I said, 'What's happening?' my mum said, 'Your dad's just put a brick through your nan's window,' which was all smashed and the brick was in the living room! That summed him up right there and then. Luckily, my mum never looked back and that was the start of our new life, thank God.

We stayed with my nan for about twelve months, I think, then we finally got a house on the other side of the town. We stayed there for about twelve months. I remember my mum working two jobs to make ends meet as a single parent, and she decided she was going to take us on our first holiday with her friend and her child too. We went on holiday and it was great. It was a Haven holiday. I remember it being fun, with lots of swimming and fun slides. But when we got back home, our house had been robbed. Sentimental things were taken, and money was taken that

Mum had saved for months! We later found out that it was my dad who had robbed us! Yes, what a scumbag, what kind of person would rob their children's home?!

Not long after that we moved back in with my nan for about two years or so, and my nan moved in with her partner round the corner. I have lots of nice memories when we were in my nan's house, like one Christmas when we got a bike each, which was a complete surprise; none of us had a clue and my mum and her current partner had hidden them in the kitchen away from the present piles. Then, after we had opened them, mum sent us in the kitchen for something, not that I can remember what now, but there they were. It was an exciting and happy Christmas that year, along with many other years too.

After a few years, my mum decided to move out of the town and we went to live in Thornton, although as I was halfway through year six, she didn't move me from my primary as there wasn't much point. I was also booked to go on a five-day PGL trip, which I was super excited about. But she did move my brothers to a different school, and my sister was in high school anyway. The PGL trip was amazing, adventurous and a trip I will remember forever, I loved every minute of it. Not long after that trip, I left the school to go onto high school. I attended my first high school for about six months on and off, but hated it. So, I asked my mum if I could move schools and she eventually said yes, which I started in year eight. The high school was called Millfield in Thornton.

Throughout my high school years, I was a shit, if I'm honest! I was gobby, I had a bad attitude and I think I thought I had to prove myself, for whatever reason, I do not know! I eventually got kicked out of high school, after being suspended three times previously. I'm not proud of the person I was back then. In fact, I wish I had knuckled down in high school and listened to the teachers. After appealing the school's decision, I eventually was accepted back into the school and given a second chance, but with one more warning: if I put a foot out of line I would be expelled on a permanent basis with no chance of appealing again. This time around I had learnt my lesson and was on my best behaviour, although I still messed about in some lessons, but not half as much as before. If I'm honest with myself, I never felt like school was for me. I have never been the academic type, more economic I'd say. I get bored very easily and still do and need to be hands on and creative, to a certain extent. I didn't put much effort into my GCSEs and, as a result, got rubbish grades and one unclassified. Therefore, I had to resit my English, maths and key skills in college. I got a C and a D in English, but didn't hand my coursework in on time for my key skills, so ended up getting the lowest grade; my own stupid fault, I know.

In the meantime, I wasn't sure what I wanted to do in life or what path I wanted to take. I'd had a few part-time jobs, my first being a chambermaid in a hotel chain. That was hard work, but I wasn't shy of it, it made time go fast, if anything. After that, I worked in a hairdressers, which was so boring I had to get out of there. Then I started working with food and really enjoyed it. This was all between the age of fourteen and sixteen. From that came my first ambition, which was to get as much experience in the catering industry and then to open my own sandwich shop by the time I was twenty-one. But let's just say that life got in the way, and I started going out at weekends clubbing with friends. That's when I met the person I was going to spend the next four years with!

I was seventeen when I met him. He was a taxi driver who I'd met once before through a younger friend of my mum's. I was in quite a vulnerable state of mind at this time in my life, as I'd not long had my heart broken for the first time, and I think he saw this from the off. I don't ever know what possessed me, but I think I was looking for someone that would maybe look after me and protect me, who knows, I still don't know. Anyway, he said he was thirty-five at the time, we started seeing each other and not long after we were a couple. About four to six months into the relationship, I found out he turned forty while I was with him and had a party at his friend's but didn't think to mention it to me and be honest, but instead hid it from me. That should have been a sign right from the start. I later forgave him and thought I loved him by this point, at the time anyway (although I can honestly say looking back it was most definitely not love!). In the meantime, my mum moved back to Fleetwood for a spell of about six months and I still lived with her. Not long after, I moved out and moved in with him at seventeen, into a shitty little flat that was scruffy and smelly, the kitchen was in the living room, the bedroom miles down the corridor and the bathroom was shared with an old man. It wasn't ideal, but it did us for a bit. I had also just come into a little money at the time and ended up funding his drug habit with most of it. I was no saint and took drugs too on occasions, usually cocaine and cannabis, yeah, great combination, I know, and I now regret this big time, but it was a learning curve in my life. Then before I knew it, the money was gone, £4000 in four months and jack shit to show apart from a few tops. It's laughable when I reflect on it!

Not long after the money had gone, we were having a heated discussion in the living room. I can't remember what about now, something pathetic, maybe money, I don't know. I remember he said something to which I replied something along the lines of, 'You fucking idiot.' As I sat down and opened my magazine, the next thing I just felt a massive bang against the right-hand side of my face and head. I was in shock and so wasn't sure what had happened, but then I realised he had smacked me from behind across my face and ear. When I turned around, he said, "Don't fucking speak to me like that ever again, do you understand me?!" At this point I was crying and screaming, 'Get out of my way,' then his guilt kicked in and he tried to stop me, but I ran and got away from him and went back to my mum's. I'm not sure how I got there, it was all a blur!

A few days after, I was in bed one night with horrific period pains. This went on all night until the following morning and, when I went to the toilet, I discovered I'd in fact had a miscarriage. I had to tell him, although he didn't have kids and said he didn't want them yet. Anyway, I forgave what he had done and went back. We moved to a more modern flat after that for a year or so then moved to a house, and then decided it was time to have a child. I fell pregnant not long after and worked until I was induced, as he had lost his cab badge, for whatever reason, I still don't know! He also hit me again during pregnancy, but I think I was so brainwashed and controlled by him that I stayed with him. Then I went back to work two weeks after having our daughter Katy. I had no choice, we had bills that needed paying and a child to feed. When I got home from work, I remember Katy was always upstairs, he'd be sitting there in the living room and it would be filled with cannabis smoke. It was as if he'd got her out of the way, so he could have a smoke, selfish prick. Three months later, I went to see the doctor and I was diagnosed with postnatal depression. When I got home, I broke down uncontrollably. I was asking for my mum, so he rang her and, when she came, I left with her and Katy; she was three months old. I revisited the house sometime after just to collect a few of Katy's things, but left everything else.

We tried to give it another go and work things out about a month later, but it was too late, the damage was done. Four years of mental and physical abuse, I had stopped loving him and I just hated him. I knew my daughter and I deserved a better life and that was the end of that. From that moment, I never looked back, and it was the best decision I ever made, especially for my daughter's future too. All I know is that I was young, dumb and VERY, VERY naïve when I got involved with an older guy, BUT I sure as fuck LEARNT FROM THIS!

At this point I was twenty-one, just, and was living with my mum with Katy, but Mum was overcrowded. So I went on the council list and eventually got a council house around the corner from her, but I hardly stayed in it as I was scared to be on my own, I suppose. After going from living with my mum until I was seventeen and then moving straight in with Katy's dad until I was twenty-one, I had never lived by myself, so it was very daunting. I started moving in gradually, as I couldn't stay with Mum forever!

Eventually, my confidence started to come back. I went on my first holiday abroad with a friend and went out on New Year's Eve for the first time in about five years. Katy was around eighteen months by then, and on that night I met friends of friends and had a good night, although my anxiety was still bad.

A few months later, it was during the world cup, I went to the local pub to watch England with a friend, where I met a friend of a friend, who I'd known of and said 'hi' to if I ever saw him about. I still remember to this day, I had never laughed as much as I did that day, because of a particular person. About two days later I received a phone call from a friend asking if she could give my number out to this person. Vinny had rung her asking to get my number off her, and after a bit of hesitation I eventually said yes. Next thing, I received a text message, saying, 'Get yaself a babysitter, I'm taking you out!' from Vinny. After chatting to my mum, I eventually replied with okay and that weekend we went on a date. Although he was hungover and hadn't had much sleep, it was still a great day and we had a great laugh, again. We found that we had so much in common, he had a son from a previous relationship, we both come from the same town, and both our parents moved out when we were eight. It was all very bizarre, but I believe, and still do to this day, of course, we were meant to be. He dropped me back at mum's in a taxi and from then we started seeing each other, as it just felt right. About four weeks later, Vinny moved in with me, and six weeks later we said those three little words. It just all felt so natural. After I had eventually introduced him to Katy, he proved to me he was good enough to be in her life too.

It wasn't all plain sailing, but we always seem to get through anything, and work it out for the better. Vinny has seen me at my lowest, when I've had breakdowns through stress from overworking myself and I've been in bed for three days or so, and he's supported me through it all and totally been there for me to comfort me, hold me and, most of all, hear me, but not just hear me, actually listen, and for that I will forever love that man wholeheartedly. I think it takes a certain kind of man to stand by his wife through those hard times. Although I didn't have a lot of respect for Vin, or men in general to be honest, in the very beginning, I have the upmost respect for him today and always will have, always and forever! That was our wedding song and will always remain true! Then, in 2011, we had our daughter, Lissie. Although I was worried about getting PND again, luckily I never did. Although I did have baby blues, but I think that's natural for any new mum. These days, I tend to deal with my anxiety and depression through running and meditation; that's my escape, or freedom, if you like. I am conscious and content when doing both, thanks to the Nike running app and Headspace app, total lifesavers. Highly recommend them both to anyone suffering with anxiety or depression or both. Mental health needs to be dealt with and we need to reach out to people who suffer, therefore we need more awareness.

When Lissie was about one, I was getting itchy feet and getting ready to get back into work, but didn't want to go back to the job I was doing in a fish and chip shop as a waitress. I wanted to pursue my ambition I had had since I was sixteen. Vinny had been in the civil service for several years, but eventually started working as a taxi driver, as a few of his friends were on the cabs too. Eventually we saw a shop to rent and we saved up for the equipment and opened up our own sandwich shop. I was so happy that I had finally pursued my dream. But this wasn't to last, as it was student-based and, when the college was closed, we just didn't take enough to compensate over the year. After about eighteen months we had to close, and I went back to my old job. I felt like a failure, but at least I had tried and given it a go, rather than to never have tried at all. Eventually, I started working online whilst holding down a part-time job and then started at university as I thought, at the time, I wanted to be a PE teacher. After one year of studying an FD in teaching and learning support, I realised this wasn't for me, but I held out another year and finished the course. I then wanted to go back to top-up my degree, but not in that subject, in something I was passionate about, which was sport and exercise.

So, after doing a bit of researching I decide to top up in Sport and Exercise Coaching. All I can say is this is where my heart lies within the health and fitness and nutrition industry. Therefore, my plans for the future are to help and educate other mothers who are feeling stuck in a rut, maybe, or even if they're feeling lonely, just like I was back then as a new mum. I felt like I was left to just get on with it, to be honest, which is understandable in a way, but at the same time very scary too. I want to help and educate other mums to find their inner confidence and know that it's okay to be feeling that way and that it's okay to talk too. I want to make other mums aware that they are not alone, and if I can do this, just by helping ONE mother, through exercise, fitness and nutrition, this will make me a very happy woman. The reason for this passion is I honestly believe that if I was made aware of this kind of thing whilst I was suffering, I may not have sunk as low as I did, or may even have recovered a little or a lot quicker! I want to be the first point of call for new mothers who have had their six-week check-ups and been given the all clear and to be recommended to give my online classes a go for free! If that's not a great offer, then I don't know what is! Great value for new mums.

16. Stacie J

★ ★ ★

I am thirty-four, I live in Blackpool, Lancashire, and I am a mum of two beautiful girls, Katy fourteen and Lissie seven, and a wife of six years, together for twelve, to the love of my life and my rock, Vinny Jones. You can reach me using the following links, to join me in my online post-natal workouts, my HiiT workouts, my blogs and vlogs too, and nutritional inspiration. Or if you're just looking for some motivation and inspiration, I'm more than happy to help.

Why not join me on my next challenge!

Instagram: https://www.instagram.com/themamafitnesscoach/

17. Katy

A nineties baby, I was born in September 1990, the eldest child in my family, followed by my brother in May 1995. My mum was an assistant bank manager at this time and my dad a mechanic. These were the times when the idea of a woman going back to work part-time to work around her child was a fantasy. I was enrolled in a nursery at four months old, as maternity leave was non-existent, and my mum and dad began paying the nursery fees – yes, they were as ridiculous then as they are now! I always remember my mum telling me how I wasn't the same child when she picked me up at 6pm, after dropping me off at 8am that morning, and that was five days a week. My parents never planned for children, so when my mum found out she was pregnant again in 1991, they made the decision for my mum to quit work and concentrate on us. Sadly, it was not meant to be, as my mum lost the baby, however she did remain at home, meaning we were very lucky to have mum at home for the whole of our childhood. We are a very small family, both my grandads passed away before I was born, and both my nans died before I turned four. Although I had aunties and uncles, we didn't really see them often, except for my mum's brother, Clive.

Anyone who knows me will agree with me when I say that I am a hugely emotional person. School friends to work colleagues, I would be very surprised to come across someone who hasn't seen me cry for one reason or another. I just can't hold it in!

At seven years old, I started experiencing what we described then as headaches. It was very hard as a seven-year-old to explain the pain. My mum would give me the recommended pain relief, but it was never enough. Numerous visits to the GP resulted in repeat eye tests, and statements like 'it's all to do with growing up', but no one would really take me seriously.

Not until I was fifteen. By this time, the 'headaches' were affecting my school work, and life in general. I remember coming home from school and not being able to move for hours. Eventually, a doctor referred me to a 'headache clinic'. By this age I was old enough to understand that these were more than headaches, and the nurse on clinic did confirm that I was experiencing migraine without aura. At the time, I was more than happy to try something to combat this invisible illness that had plagued the last eight years of my life. Initially I was prescribed a low dose beta blocker, and advised to take Migraleve, which is now an over-the-counter painkiller.

In 2006, I met the love of my life. Martin (Mart) is now my husband and we have been together for twelve years and married for four. I passed my GCSEs with ten As and Bs, but after some consideration I decided to leave my A Levels and get a job. All I wanted at this time was to earn money, to contribute to household costs as, by the time I was seventeen, I had moved in with Mart. My parents were hugely supportive of my choice to move out and I spoke to my mom twice a day every day – I missed home lots, but I would never let on!

In June 2008, I started working for NatWest (Royal Bank of Scotland) as a customer service advisor; my first ever taste of full-time work, where I thought my adventure would begin!

By this time, I had tried several medications for my migraines, none of which made a difference and, as I quickly learned, the pressure of full-time work only made matters worse. At seventeen years old, with no experience of working in a bank or with large amounts of cash for that matter, I found myself sitting at a cashier's desk after two weeks of training! I cringe at the thought now, but then I was a very naïve teenager.

Days would consist of hefty customer queues, taking hundreds of thousands of pounds in cash, being verbally abused by irate customers, and days ending with my till being thousands of pounds wrong. I would spend hours in tears as money was missing, simply because I had pressed a deposit button rather than a withdrawal button. The pressure was immense, and my health worsened.

I remember an occasion where I walked into work on day twelve of a migraine. I woke up with it and went to sleep with it, no painkillers in the world would kill the bugger! It wasn't very often I experienced sickness, but this migraine was filled with fury. The queue was out of the door, and due to my till errors, I was being observed by management – great, more stress! I was refused permission to leave my seat and was forced to gag into a waste paper bin in full view of the customers; how humiliating! A wiser, older me would have showed the manager the birdy and run to the bathroom, but at seventeen I didn't have an ounce of courage, and I had no idea what was right or wrong.

By 2010, after trying a range of medications and not having any success and being refused any kind of investigations, my mum arranged a private consultation. My mum's eldest brother died from a spontaneous brain haemorrhage in 1999, and she needed peace of mind that there was nothing seriously wrong with me. I had an MRI scan and all was clear; this doctor took me on as his NHS patient at another local hospital.

I will always remember being quite upset in one consultation with my consultant as none of the medications were making an ounce of difference and life was pretty dismal. The response to my forceful questions was, 'God gave you migraine, and I (the doctor) am just here to fix it.'

So, as a nineteen-year-old who was failing at employment, having only an average of ten days a month pain free, I was supposed to blame God?? Where do these doctors get off?

So, in August 2010, after leaving NatWest and planning for my career, I landed a job as a trainee dental nurse in the NHS. I won't even pretend to make you believe I liked it, it was bloody awful. But, I do have two reasons that I am glad I did it. It gave me a door into the NHS and it gave me an NVQ, which helped me get on further in life.

It was another job filled with migraines and anxiety, sitting in the train station car park in the car, frozen to the seat, filled with dread, sobbing on the phone to my mum. No one understood. The sickness meetings and threats of dismissal resurfaced and in turn new meds, higher doses and more pain killers.

What I knew by this time was that the painkillers were actually causing more problems than good. I had been advised of 'analgesic overuse', which is when repetitive consumption of painkillers can actually cause headaches rather than helping the migraine. The problem is, this is a very difficult issue to solve, I needed the meds to get through the day.

I completed my NVQ in 2012 and couldn't get out of there quick enough. I found a job in a small dental practice. I was fully aware by now that my medical condition made holding down a standard nine to five job very difficult. So, I decided to start up my own little business. This was my first ever experience of being self-employed. I still needed the full-time job as we couldn't rely on one income, so I prepared myself to work weekends providing children's parties as well as in the week. All I could think of was the possibility that someday I could be my own boss and not have to sit through another sickness review!

From 2012, I was also visiting my mum's brother, Uncle Clive, every weekend to help out. He was always a very independent man, but as his health worsened, he needed someone to do bits and bobs for him; it was lovely, and I loved him dearly. I lasted six months in the practice and walked out one lunchtime never to return. The one and only time I have ever done that, and I can admit I am not proud, but it really does show my mindset at the time.

Things were bad. The hospital had prescribed some anti-epileptic drugs to try and control my migraines. I was taking 3000mg of these drugs per day, which was nine tablets; I was only twenty-two. It's only now I'm writing this that I can see how my life could have ended up on the wrong path. I have no idea how I didn't become addicted to prescription painkillers, what I do know and remember well is the morning I spent driving to another new job, sobbing to my mum on the car phone, telling her I wanted to end it all and I wanted to drive my car off the road as everything would be better. That day I had a breakdown in the new job and they asked me to leave and not return.

I spent the next three months weaning myself off the drugs and painkillers, speaking to doctors about alternatives that didn't involve medication. I was still running my little business, which averaged fifty-two parties a year. In January 2013 I started working in the NHS as an assistant audiologist. This job showed me that there is support and that work can be enjoyable. I secured funding for a new innovative migraine therapy, which consisted of Botox injections into my skull and forehead along with some into my jaw. The therapy worked, and my migraine frequency drastically reduced. My job gave me confidence and made me strong, I really loved the people I worked with and I am sure every one of them has seen me cry; let's just say, since 2013 there have been plenty of reasons to cry!

I worked my party business alongside my full-time job for three and a half years. I loved it and bookings were flying in. This was the first time I had used social media for business, and very soon bookings were coming in through word of mouth. Mart and I booked our wedding and my little business paid for a good chunk of it! I've always been a very creative person and I can put my mind to anything, my wedding was no exception. I designed and made all the stationery, bouquets and favours, which made the day so much more special.

I had been going to see my uncle Clive every Sunday, getting his bits and bobs from Sainsburys and having the odd baking competition. I'm sure he cheated one week and bought those cookies from the shop! One Sunday morning I was due to visit, I had been to my work's Christmas do the evening before, and I was due to do a party that afternoon. My mum and I knew before I even got to his flat, I have no idea how or why we knew, but something just wasn't right. Martin and I arrived and there was no answer at the door. It was locked, which was unusual when he was expecting me. We gained entry and found him in a peaceful forever sleep. I was heartbroken, and I miss him so much. All the lovely things he has missed, we can only hope he is looking down watching.

We got married on the 20th September 2014. It was the most magical day and I loved every second of it. Two days later we jetted off to Florida for our honeymoon.

The day we were flying back was the day everything changed. Packing the cases, Mart came out of the bathroom as white as a sheet; he said my mum had just called him. This was very odd, as my mum would never call anyone but me. Then he had to tell me that my dad had suffered a stroke and he was in hospital, that he was alive, but things weren't looking good. We flew home and rushed to the hospital. The first time I saw my dad I was sure he was going to die. The doctors explained that his carotid artery on the right side of his neck was totally blocked and therefore starving the blood flow to his brain. Until this day, my dad was working full-time as a marine engineer. The man I saw in the hospital bed was struggling to speak and had no idea what had happened to him. In the following days, it was apparent that my dad could no longer walk; he had no use at all of his left arm or hand and the stroke had also taken his ability to swallow. Doctors had no idea what to do for the best. Initial plans to give dad a drug to disperse the clot were dismissed as it could cause haemorrhage. They fitted a naso-gastric tube to feed dad and gave him physiotherapy to help bring back his swallowing. Slowly, he was moved onto a puree diet. I visited every evening after work to feed dad soup and yogurts, as the food the hospital served was awful.

Dad couldn't go home to his and mum's house, as he couldn't walk. The house just wasn't adapted for his needs. So, all of us made the decision to live together, Mart and I left our rented house, while mum and dad sold the family home. We found a property where dad could live downstairs and both my brother and I were around to help out. Dad came out of hospital on the 23rd December 2014 and started to walk with a stick in April 2015. It's taken hours of physiotherapy and many hospital appointments, but dad is starting to adapt to life with significant disabilities. It's safe to say that when we found out that we were expecting Niamh in April 2016, everyone was grateful for some positive news.

We fell pregnant after six months of trying and were ecstatic when we found out. I felt super lucky as I hadn't had any morning sickness; actually I felt better than ever! Later in the pregnancy wasn't as smooth. I was diagnosed with gestational diabetes at twenty weeks, and I suffered with SPD and sciatica from around the same time. I couldn't wait to get her out!

At thirty-eight weeks, Mart rushed me into hospital and they confirmed I had pre-eclampsia – it was a rollercoaster. I was induced (horrific experience), I had an epidural that didn't work and I collapsed in the shower from blood loss… but I had a beautiful baby girl on the 25th March 2016 weighing 7lbs 7oz. She was perfect – and still is, but I'm biased!

When Niamh was six months old, I really didn't like the idea of going back to my job in the NHS; I loved the job, but I wanted more. So, I applied to my local university to study a BA(Hons) in Education Studies and started in September 2016; that seems like a lifetime ago… yet I graduate in seven months!

I never wanted a big age gap between my children, so in July 2017 we decided to try for the next. I was positive that I could manage my final year of university with a newborn. We got pregnant really quickly and I found out our baby was due 15th April 2018. Then in mid-September I started bleeding; the GP reassured me this can be normal but booked me an early scan to be sure. We went for our scan on our wedding anniversary and, while we sat and waited, we both looked at each other and knew that things were not going to be the same once we went into that room.

The sonographer scanned in silence, then the question I was dreading: 'Are your dates right? Are you sure you're ten weeks along?' There was no heartbeat, our baby had stopped growing at six weeks.

I was then asked to 'clean up' and sit in another room. It was the room of sadness, the room of nothing, a room to cry. A nurse came to tell us that we had to wait a fortnight before the hospital could provide any intervention and the only hope I had was that my body would realise my baby had died and start the process itself. On the 23rd September 2017 we lost our baby.

I was devastated. My mum understood, but no one else seemed to. I had all the normal comments, 'it wasn't meant to be', 'there will be another' – funny that… I don't want another! The best one: 'it's mother nature's way'.

In January 2018, as a way to fill the emptiness, I started sewing. I liked the idea of keeping busy (as if a degree and a two-year-old isn't enough?) and the chance to maybe earn a few pennies. I had made myself a nappy wallet when Niamh was small and some for friends, but I knew I wasn't happy with my design. I reworked my design and popped them on Facebook. I was overwhelmed at the response, orders started coming in and the feedback was awesome. I named the business 'Niamh's Neverland' and it has been a whirlwind ten months. I have topped 270 orders, made over 350 products, developed new lines, secured a stand at a national exhibition next month (November 2018) and have wholesale contracts in the pipeline. The other day someone said my little angel is looking over me; all I know is that my experiences have definitely pushed me to take a leap, and the experience of loss and pain has helped build me into the person I am today.

★ ★ ★

Katy is twenty-eight years old, mummy to Niamh and owner of Niamh's Neverland. Her fabulous collection of pretty, practical accessories can be found at www.niamhsneverland.com

18. Kim

I grew up in a large city, San Jose, California. I had an uneventful childhood with a religious Christian family, a stay-at-home mom, four sisters and one brother. There is an age split between us, and my youngest sister was born when I was fourteen and in middle school. I was so proud to carry this little baby in my arms when I walked into ninth grade orientation. When I was ten, my family moved from California to a suburb of Salt Lake City, Utah. This was an age when I was excited to move and explore a new place, meet new friends and play in the snow! I was in sixth grade and met a few friends that would change my life for the better. I made a new friend that would leave our classroom to go learn in another class. I asked her why she would leave and where she went. She told me she had dyslexia and was going to another classroom to learn. She said it was fun and the teacher was so nice to her! I knew then that I wanted to help students with learning challenges.

At sixteen, I loved school, had a lot of friends, and enjoyed my beautiful home. I was a teenager who did not break any rules. I always listened to my parents and at times even went to bed early by choice. My parents did not have a lot of money, but I never realised we were not wealthy as we had everything we needed, modest Christmases, and were taught gratitude and service. As an adult, I realised all that was sacrificed for my mom to be home with us. I noticed that I always needed a lot of sleep; even more than other teens needed. This was also the time I was doing well in school, yet I was calling my mom every day from school to pick me up from having a stomachache and headaches. I knew I wasn't avoiding school and, thankfully, my mom believed me. This started many tests to determine what was causing my symptoms: nausea, fatigue, stomach pain, joint pain and blurred vision. By the age of twenty-one, I would be diagnosed with Crohn's Disease, a chronic illness with no cure and chronic migraines.

In 2001, I married a man that shared my same religion. I truly believed if I lived righteously and was a good wife, all my dreams would come true of having my family attend church together, and that we would buy a home, and have money in the bank for a rainy day. We would be able to raise healthy children and I could be a stay-at-home mom, or work because I wanted to and not because I was worried about making enough money and paying bills. My dream would not happen yet as there wasn't enough money and I needed to support our family. Since I needed to work, I began teaching in a school, educating children with disabilities. This was a passion of mine as it was a way for me to teach them differently, finding a way to help them to love learning. I made amazing connections with my students. It was also at this time that I had my son. He was such a blessing to us. When I was growing up, I only wanted to be two things, a special education teacher, and a mom. It seemed like I had accomplished both of those goals.

However, to my dismay, the man I married struggled with addictions and was verbally abusive. I wanted to leave several times but believed that if I kept my faith and relied on God, I would be able to endure this rough time and we could continue to be a family. We went to counselling and tried to work through our marital issues. Our problems would always improve, but solutions seemed to only be temporary. We attempted to prioritise our family and do more together. We were living in Las Vegas and my husband decided he wanted to relocate our family to Colorado. I was happy with our home and our friends where we lived but decided that if this would help our family stay together then it was worth the move. I began applying for jobs and was fortunate enough to receive the first one I was interested in. With our move to Colorado also came a fresh start for my family. We moved in August of 2006 and a couple of months later found out our first daughter was on the way. This was a joyous time and we had a focus of being able to buy a house to bring our daughter home.

We achieved our goal of buying a home in Colorado. In 2010, another little girl blessed our family. She came at a time when everything was chaotic. Her birth was very special as she was born on my mom's birthday, my nephew was born the same day, and it was also the day we found out my mom's cancer was in remission. She was a busy little baby from the minute she was born. She was the perfect caboose to complete our family. Later that year, I got really sick. My Crohn's disease had advanced to where I needed to have surgery and have part of my small intestine removed. This was not something I wanted to do, but I knew I didn't have an option if I wanted to feel better and stay healthy. I was scared, and my baby was only six months old. I also had a husband that was always travelling for work, which left me in a single mom position also working forty hours a week teaching. I had the surgery and healed up well. Unfortunately, my disease returned rapidly. It was so aggressive, I ended up having the same surgery again eighteen months later in May of 2012. I was assured this surgery would heal me. In August of 2012, I found out that my disease had returned aggressively again.

With my current stressful, busy lifestyle, I knew that I needed to make a change due to increased aggression from my then husband, my declining health and longing to ensure the ongoing abuse no longer had an impact on my children. My husband and I were not good together. I got up the courage and filed for divorce from my children's father and felt a huge weight come off my shoulders. My Crohn's Disease went into remission. My doctor suspected it was in remission because I was internalising a lot of stress, which kept my illness active and destroying my intestines. With the divorce being finalised in early 2013, I felt free and was able to rebuild my life, or so I thought.

About one year after my marriage ended, I was searching to be loved, cared for and to find a partner to help raise my children. It was then that I reconnected with a man from my past. My family soon shared our religion with his family and they were converted. He and I had always had a crush on each other when we were pre-teens but had never pursued it. At that time, I didn't realise how he would manipulate me, steal from me and destroy my possessions, all while being high on methamphetamine. This marriage began in the summer of 2014 and had ended by December of 2014 with him pushing me down wooden stairs and pinning me against the wall while choking me. Thankfully my children were with their father at the time, as I have never screamed so loudly in my life. While he was choking me, I remember the anger in his eyes as he stared into mine. I couldn't breathe and all I could think about was how I was going to escape. When I got loose from his grip, I grabbed my keys and ran out to my car, shoeless, braless, and in pyjamas. I fumbled with my keys to unlock the car door with only seconds before he would catch me. With his monstrous frame chasing me, I was unsure if I would be able to escape. I prayed for my neighbours to call the police or come out and help, but it was a dark, silent night. I was able to get in my car, locked my doors, and was able to start it up. As I reversed out of the driveway crying and shaking, this large man pounded on my window and windshield trying to break in to get to me. I have never been so terrified, then or now. I didn't know where to go or what to do, so I called my mom. She met me at a gas station and helped me find a place to stay where I could not be found. It was then I saw the unconditional love my family had for me. They rallied around me to ensure my safety and well-being. I will be forever grateful my children were not home to witness what had happened. Later, I filed physical abuse felony charges against my second husband for stalking, harassment, and extortion.

During this time, I was also being taken to court by my ex-husband for money issues regarding child support. It was the hardest six months of my entire life. I stopped sleeping because every time I would close my eyes, I would have flashbacks and nightmares about being killed, each night in a different, violent way. I had now been a victim of domestic violence more than once. My life had been derailed and there was nothing I could do to stop it; I was alone, scared, beaten down. Everyone encouraged me to call the police and press criminal charges in order to stop him, but before I did, I was scared he would find out and hurt me even more. Statistics worked against me; one in three women in my position are killed by the other party if police are involved. I just wanted to be left alone; live my life without looking back. He kept threatening to post pictures of me on the internet unless I paid him money. I did not know he had pictures of me, so I ignored him, until he started texting me pictures he actually had. I was so terrified and didn't know what to do. I ended up paying him, so he would stop, but instead of stopping, the texts I received were more threatening. He threatened to kill me if I said anything. He was texting my friends and family with lies. He hacked my social media accounts, email accounts, financial accounts; anything he could get his hands on. I ended up going to the police about one month later.

I suffered physically by losing over 50lbs, looking like a frail shell of myself. I was pale and throwing up frequently from stress and anxiety. I was forced to leave my home. He had said the following to me, which are words I will never forget, "One day, you will open your front door and someone will shoot you in the face. You won't know what hit you because it won't be me. It will be one of my friends that already has your picture and address." These words pierced my soul. I decided that day I would move in with my parents and sell that house. I was continuing to work forty hours per week as a special education teacher, raising my three children, and living with my parents for safety reasons. This was also the time period I was diagnosed with post-traumatic stress disorder (PTSD) and started medication prescribed by my psychiatrist. I lived every day fearful he would find me, isolated from the world since I couldn't go anywhere alone, and hopeless about ever finding a new normal for myself and children. I would do anything to change to a different path, have a new life and move on from the past two destructive relationships. This marriage did end up being annulled in the Spring of 2015.

I testified in criminal court against him on 1st June, 2015. He pleaded guilty and asked for a lighter sentence. The judge granted his request. I felt defeated and exhausted from his minimal consequence. I felt as though the judge made the best choice for him, discounting all I had said and tossing my safety aside. I will never forget her words, "At some point, you become a menace to society, but I'm going to give you another chance." Another chance? This man had multiple felony convictions. I was risking my life testifying against him. How could this be? Even though he was minimally sentenced, I was still glad I made my voice heard to stand up for myself and help other women to protect themselves more than I had. The sentence had him supervised for five years, which meant no other woman would be harmed during that time. I felt peace knowing I had made an impact that way. He ended up only being supervised for three years, but three years of safety for others is still better than nothing.

From this difficult time in my life, I found a loving, accepting domestic violence support group, an amazing therapist to help me heal, and a huge support system from my family and friends. I was going to not only survive, but I knew I was also going to thrive!

And thrive I did! I rebuilt my life. I bought a home in the winter of 2016 on my own. I completed my administrator degree for becoming a principal in the public school system. My children were safe and happy. I started dating an incredible, kind and loving man. A man I had no clue would stand by my side in health and the sickness that was to come. My life was on track, until January of 2017, when I felt a hard, golf ball sized lump in my left breast, only a month and a half after seeing my doctor for an annual breast exam. I started investigating this lump by seeing my doctor and she told me to not be worried. She said a phrase to the effect of how she had felt thousands of women's breasts and my lump felt normal, soft, and not to worry about it. She offered to schedule a mammogram to ease my mind that the lump truly was nothing. That began my battle with my health insurance company and doctors to get a mammogram. Why would it be a battle for a routine test, you ask? Well, it took four phone calls because the doctor entered the order in the computer wrong. On the fourth phone call, I was ready to give up. I geared up for another battle and a kind woman answered, heard my story, and assured me she would get the orders corrected to have my mammogram completed. This woman followed through with her promise and scheduled the correct mammogram. After it, my medical team told me to get a biopsy if I wanted, but there was no need to rush. So, I didn't rush. I had my mammogram at the beginning of February. I scheduled my biopsy at the end of March to ease my mind. The best scenario would be a benign, non-cancerous growth, worst-case scenario would be cancer. I was optimistic, though, as the doctor wasn't concerned, and I was only thirty-six years old.

My life forever changed after that biopsy. 29th March, 2017 will be a day I never forget. My life halted. Time stood still and my whole body was numb as I received the devastating news: "You have breast cancer, it is aggressive, and you need to plan on one to two years of active cancer treatments." I was flabbergasted, frightened and worried about my children, my new home, my life.

I was diagnosed in March 2017 and had a whirlwind of cancer

treatments starting with a bilateral mastectomy, which determined my tumour had spread to my breast bone. Then, treatment followed with one year of chemotherapy (seventeen total treatments), a full hysterectomy in December of 2017, and reconstruction breast surgery in February 2018.

All the while my health crisis was going on, I decided to not ever be dependent on working outside of my home to get a paycheck. I decided it was time to build multiple sources of income for myself and family and began building my essential oils business in November 2017. From that date on, I was successful with sharing essential oils and living a less toxic lifestyle. Building my essential oils business was pivotal for me as I truly believe my cancer was caused from stress and toxins in my life. I was passionate about essential oils and knew I could help educate others on limiting toxins in their homes and around their families. I was also able to bring my art of teaching into my business, so it was a win-win situation. I am still building my business, but plan on my essential oils becoming my primary income in the next two years.

I am now a cancer survivor, entrepreneur, and mommy of an athletic teenage son and two musically-gifted girls, eleven and eight. My life has been forever changed by my past and I would dare say for the better! I now try to find the positive in everything and keep an optimistic outlook. When you have wondered if you're going to live and survive, so many other things become irrelevant. The stressors that would keep me up at night worried no longer have an impact on my life. I'm a constant work in progress, as we all are, but for the most part, cancer blessed my life to give me the opportunity to live whatever life I choose. Cancer showed me how short life really is. This is my new beginning, which not everyone is afforded. I intend to spend the rest of my days living by the Golden Rule, helping my children thrive in our society, and continuing to bless others' lives with educating on the benefits of daily use of essential oils.

Dream big and follow that dream! You can be anything you want to be, no matter your age! Live the life you want! Do the next right thing. Become that woman you've always imagined because you can. Remember to love yourself, spoil yourself, and make yourself a priority!

18. Kim

Kim Williams is a thirty-eight-year-old single mom to three kind children, Bryce, Zoe and Ellie. They reside in Denver, Colorado. She has recently battled breast cancer and is currently cancer-free! She's an avid essential oil user and loves to learn about how oils can heal your entire body systems from physical to mental health. Kim loves to educate families on eliminating toxins from their homes.

Follow Kim on IG for non-toxic tips and tricks for your lifestyle at: https://www.instagram.com/oil_sparklers/

19. Sarah

Born in the late 1970s, I am the eldest of four girls. We lived in a big house and I have happy memories of my childhood; I loved having so many sisters. Aged thirteen, I really wanted to join the army when I was old enough, and aged sixteen I completed my tests to join up and passed. Then in January 1995 I was officially in The British Army. I completed my training, had my first posting and fitted so well into squaddie life, I loved it.

After seven years and receiving two medals for tours, I bought my first home and decided to leave the army. I struggled to adjust to civilian life for the first few years and suffered with depression and, at one point, wanted to end it all. It was hard to make friends, and the friends I already had just weren't on the same level as me. But things got better, and I met my son's dad.

It took us a while to get pregnant but in 2006 my 9lb 1oz gorgeous baby boy was born. The first year was hard; I suffered post-natal depression and my son had an undiagnosed dairy intolerance for six months. By the time he was two, I noticed that something wasn't quite right. I thought he was deaf; he didn't even mumble and had never spoken. He would stare blankly, and we just couldn't communicate with him at all. I took him for a hearing test, positive he had glue ear and that he couldn't hear a thing. At the appointment, the doctor told me that his hearing was perfect, but she had done another assessment of him and thought something else was going on, possibly autism. I wasn't expecting that at all.

As the years went on, I struggled to understand how to help my son. He didn't have a full diagnosis yet, but he was diagnosed at first with severe language delay. No support was around, and I learnt from other mums in my situation, and local National Autistic Society support groups helped so much. My son started school in an inclusion base and shortly after had another diagnosis of learning difficulties. The base was amazing as it was a smaller class with lots of one-to-one help. He would have bad meltdowns, and was very hypersensitive. During a meltdown in public, I would just have to block out everyone's glares and comments and just make sure he stayed safe. He wouldn't recognise me and scream for his mum; I couldn't touch him, and it was truly heartbreaking to see him like this. Aged six my son was diagnosed with a condition called bilateral anterior uveitis; he would have his pupils dilated twenty-four hours a day, along with steroid drops, he also wore Polarised glasses inside as well as outside. Around the same time, he was diagnosed with ADHD, and it was decided he didn't have autism. So, his diagnoses were severe language delay, learning difficulties, ADHD, dyslexia and chronic bilateral uveitis.

In September 2013 I was diagnosed with a pituitary tumour. I sat in the consultant's room with my friend and suddenly it seemed like I wasn't there, like I was listening from outside the room; it was a huge shock. My mum had been diagnosed with the same tumour a few years earlier. Not long after my diagnosis, one of my sisters also had the diagnosis of the same tumour! After being told for years 'No we won't do a brain MRI because it's not genetic', my mum, my sister and I had all been diagnosed.

Fast forward a few years and I really wanted another child. I had three sisters and didn't want my son to be an only child, I wanted him to have a brother or sister, and he kept begging me for one. Only thing was I was single, happy and single, and not the type to get into relationships. I had thought of this idea for a while and now decided to make it happen.

I was infertile by this point due to my tumour, as my hormones weren't behaving as they should be, so I was never getting pregnant, or so I thought. I was under the infertility clinic and had a procedure in the November, and three weeks later found out I was pregnant.

A week later, three days before Christmas, my son woke up and said he couldn't see me. We immediately drove to hospital, and when we arrived, I noticed I had started bleeding. My mum, sister and my son's dad came over to the hospital; my son was having so many tests done, and my bleeding was getting worse, and I would have to travel to a different hospital to get checked over. I had to leave my son with my family, so I could find out what was happening with my pregnancy. My baby was fine, I could see him or her still there. I felt relief and rushed back to see my son. His diagnosis wasn't good. He now had bilateral pan uveitis/choroiditis, all the layers from front to back in both eyes and could permanently lose his vision. He stayed in hospital over Christmas and was allowed home for three hours on Christmas day, but went back early as he felt so ill. He was pumped with lots of steroids and other medicines and came home with his vision improved a lot. January 2015, he started methotrexate tablets and sickness tablets both once a week, but he was so ill from vomiting that he was changed onto injections. I wasn't allowed to handle them to administer them because I was pregnant and it's a cytotoxic drug, so his dad was taught how to do it. Every Friday night he would have that injection, and though not as bad as the tablets, he didn't feel well each weekend.

At eight weeks pregnant I went to have another scan just because of the bleeding and was very surprised to find out that my one baby was two babies, twins in two different sacs. Panic set in; how would I manage with two babies and my son going through his treatment? After a week or so, I was so excited and felt really blessed to be having two new arrivals that year. We were visiting hospital one to two times a week for my son to be checked out, and early pregnancy with twins, and because I was bleeding, put me under a lot of stress. One day before my twelve-week scan, the bleeding became heavier and my sister drove me to A&E, where on the bed I bled everywhere, so much blood that I knew I had lost my twins. I was distraught and had to wait two hours before they finally scanned me. Both babies' heartbeats were fine, and they were both waving at me; I couldn't believe my eyes, we had all been through so much in eight weeks.

At twenty-one weeks, I didn't feel so good. I was so tired and had a strange feeling something wasn't right. I took some time off work and I visited the midwife, and everything was fine. The following morning, lying in bed, I remembered the wheelie bins were getting collected, so made my way downstairs, went up my drive with the bin, walked back inside, towards the kitchen and that's when my waters broke. I was twenty-two weeks pregnant. I called my mum and sister, stuck a towel down my pjs between my legs, woke my son up, gave him breakfast and then the school transport picked him up.

We went over to hospital where I found I had PPROM, Preterm premature rupture of the membranes, and that I could go into labour at any time. I had steroid injections and cried solidly. I had to stay in hospital until my babies were born. The doctors came around with some forms for me to sign; they would come each week with the forms. These forms were our agreement on what to do that week if the babies arrived, resuscitate them, not resuscitate them, etc., and I made a tough decision that at twenty-two weeks, if they came, to just give pain relief. The tubes would have been too big for their tiny bodies and I didn't want to hurt them further. At twenty-four weeks I could finally say yes to save my babies and do everything possible. When I reached twenty-six weeks, I could be monitored on the machine each day, something myself and the other girls in my room all celebrated with a Chinese takeaway party.

Twenty-eight weeks arrived, and I really wasn't feeling good. I had baby poo coming out, but was told it was only a tiny amount and not to worry. I had the runs, terrible back pain, which I thought was early labour, but still told no it's just the weight from the babies. I was ignored, the professionals knew better, and I was just a silly pregnant lady. My pleas to scan and have more tests were ignored; even when I started bleeding a little, the consultant told me my babies were fine and if he thought anything was about to happen, he would do something. Literally a few hours later I walked into the bathroom and suddenly the whole floor was covered in my blood, I was screaming, the other two pregnant ladies in my room trying to help me, also screaming for help. One midwife came in, saw the blood and said she was calling the on-call doctor and would be back in a minute. Five minutes later, she came with a wheelchair; unable to get hold of the doctor, she was taking me to the delivery suite. The other pregnant ladies held the door open for her and I could see about five other midwives laughing, having a tea break at the nurse's station; not one came to help me, or the other midwife, or to console the other pregnant ladies, or to close off the bathroom to be cleaned. I had more steroid injections in the delivery suite as my babies weren't due for another three months.

I was in the delivery suite from the Tuesday night up until the Friday afternoon, bleeding, a lot. I was constantly on the monitor and my family stayed with me most of the time. Each morning, the doctor would examine me internally and say, 'Yes there's blood, but it'll be okay for now.' On the Friday morning a different consultant came to examine me, and said I need to have my babies by c-section in a few hours. I was put on a magnesium infusion and then taken to theatre. I was scared yet excited to meet my babies; I was told they were both doing fine. The theatre had about twenty people in there, a team for each baby and lots of other people. I had my epidural and my mum sat beside me, the screen up so we couldn't see what was happening. I think the scariest thing at that moment was all the people in the room watching, waiting to help my babies. I knew to expect them to need help with breathing, but I felt confident that everything would run smoothly.

I could swear that I heard a baby cry, but then it stopped; then I was told twin one was born at 3.01pm, big huge smiles appeared on mine and my mum's face; then at 3.03pm twin two was born. Twin one I named Teddy Adam William and twin two Tilly Ann, my beautiful twins Teddy and Tilly. Teddy weighed 2lbs 12oz and Tilly weighed 2lb 5oz.

Everyone was busy doing their jobs in theatre and the main consultant was watching over everything. An incubator came to my side with five people around it. I was introduced to my daughter Tilly. I couldn't touch her and she had been ventilated at birth; they said they needed to take her straight to intensive care to be cared for. After she left, I asked one of the doctors if they would also show me my son before he went to intensive care too, but they told me he had already gone out of another door. I look back now and I didn't seem too concerned at the time, I thought that's just what happens. I was taken to recovery, but my mum wasn't allowed to come back in; she went to go and see my babies. It seemed like hours in recovery and nobody could give me any updates on my babies, even the consultant walked past me and didn't say anything. By this time I was getting quite anxious because I had no family with me, I was alone, and my babies were in intensive care.

After about ninety minutes, I was allowed to leave recovery. I was pushed on my bed to meet my mum in a room. My sisters were with my babies, they were both in separate intensive care rooms. A nurse told me we could go around to see Tilly. I was wheeled in and sat up in my bed next to her incubator. She was tiny, the size of my hand, she had tubes in her mouth, lots of tubes in her belly button, covered in monitoring equipment but was a healthy pink colour. I was so in love with this little fighter. I asked to see Teddy, but was told they were still trying to stabilise him and I would need to wait a little longer. They finally wheeled me round to his unit and, as we approached the door, they asked the nurse to take me to the ward. I was confused and very worried, I just wanted to see my little boy, to make sure he was okay.

We arrived at the ward and ten minutes later I was allowed to meet my son. I was taken into his intensive care unit. The other parents had been asked to leave, and a privacy curtain put up around our area. A doctor was doing chest compressions on Teddy while a professor told me that my son had a bleed on the brain, that they had done a second scan and it was getting worse. He had had two blood transfusions but was losing too much blood. The other doctor stopped compressions and he seemed stable. The professor told me they had tried two different types of ventilator, and the current one is for extremely poorly babies, and wasn't working very well for Teddy. Then all of a sudden doctors were pressing on his chest again, his chest was black from bruising, his ribs broken, he was almost blue, he had blood coming from his mouth and ears, he was very poorly. I shouted, 'STOP!' I told them to stop trying to help him. It was mother's instinct, I didn't want my baby to suffer anymore, they had tried to bring him back nine times by then, and I couldn't let it go on anymore. They stopped, and I told them to pass him to me. They took his ventilator off and placed him on my chest. Instantly I put his mouth to my nipple, and I squeezed some breast milk onto his tiny lips, I wanted him to smell and feel me, know I was there for him. Teddy passed away moments later, on my chest at 6.01pm, cuddled by his mummy, while his grandma and three aunties watched over. My sister captured the moment on camera and I'm so grateful that I have that memory to look back on at any time.

My son had died, my daughter was fighting for her life and my eldest son was on his way to the hospital to meet them both; my world fell apart, I didn't know what to do, or how to tell my son. We were taken to a private room with Teddy where I just cuddled and cuddled him, completely heartbroken. My eldest son went straight to meet his sister and then his dad brought him in to see me. Teddy was in his little cot at that point. My nine-year-old son asked when he could go and see his brother. I pulled him up on my bed, cuddled him and somehow told him that his little brother had died. His heartache almost killed me, this is the worst moment ever in my whole life. My mum passed Teddy to me and I gently laid him in my son's arms. He cuddled his little brother, sobbing his heart out. I cuddled them both, trying to be brave for all my children. I couldn't protect my son from his heartache and seeing him go through this is the worst part of this whole story.

I stayed in hospital for five more days. It was a bank holiday weekend and the bereavement team didn't work weekends or bank holiday Mondays! So Teddy stayed with me for the five days. The first night I dressed my son in his tiny clothes and kissed every part of his body; he had a cool cot and I tucked him in and watched him. Twelve hours after my daughter was born, I went back round to see her. I was absolutely heartbroken, yet over the moon, having just lost one baby but also having a newborn little girl to be happy about.

Three weeks later, I buried my son Teddy. My eldest son wanted to lift his coffin into the ground with me; it was important to him to be a part of it all. This was another heartbreaking yet very proud moment.

Over the next nine weeks, we visited my daughter every day, an hour round trip twice a day, in between picking my son up from school. She had my breastmilk and started off on half a ml, and at nine weeks old came home off oxygen.

We moved house when she was four months old and after that we could finally start trying to get our family life back to normal. My daughter has a few health problems and spent a lot of time in hospital over the following years, and I left my job at the hospital because she was ill a lot.

In 2017, I decided to start my business, working from home, whilst being able to care for my children and make a living. I took my past experiences with special educational needs and disabilities and created The Sensory Fairy, helping other parents find sensory solutions for their children.

When I look back through my story, I feel heartache but also pride, as a family we have endured so much over the last few years, I could easily have given up, but fought through everything instead, for my children and for myself. When people say time is a healer, I used to think what a load of rubbish, but now I truly believe in this. The most important goal for me is to make my children happy and to be proud of what their mother can achieve.

★ ★ ★

Sarah is a forty-one-year-old proud mother to Owen and Tilly, and Teddy who sadly passed away in 2015.
She created her award-winning business, The Sensory Fairy, to be able to help other parents who find themselves in a similar situation with a child who has special educational needs and/or disabilities, to provide sensory equipment, toys and resources, which she calls sensory solutions.
Sarah has a wonderful website with lots of resources, and you can find them all at www.thesensoryfairy.com

20. Lorraine

As a little child, my memories of my mum are quite vague. You see, my mum was and still is an alcoholic. She was only in my life until I was seven. My memories of her weren't always happy either, I remember the times she used to beat us at a strange hour. I have nine brothers and sisters and we all shared beds, the girls in one room, Mum, Dad and baby in another, and the lads in another. Things were okay until Christmas Eve night when I was seven. Mum told my dad she was leaving him for some bloke who'd got three kids. That night Dad had a heart attack and was hospitalised. What happened after that I've no memory of, I just remember my baby brother being dumped outside in the garden.

Primary school became bad. I was called 'smelly, ugly, tramp', that sort of thing. My teacher would take me into the toilets and sit me in the sink and wash me. One of my teachers even took me home and clothed me. I left primary and started secondary school. Wow that was a shock! Nobody had told me what to expect or what it would be like. Yep, and I was even bullied again. I ended up playing truant most of the twelve months I was there. My dad told us we were moving to a bigger house and in a nicer area.

Money and food were scarce a lot of the time, but my dad was doing the best he could with what he had. The bullying stopped at my new school and I made some lovely friends. My sister always said, 'Never let anyone hit you, stand up for yourself,' so I did and most days at school I got the cane. By the time I was ready to leave school I was not prepared for exams. I'd truanted quite a lot. I managed three and passed them, but that was it. I found it hard not having a mum around, I think. I was braless for years until I was about fifteen or so. My dad embarrassed me in the shop, so I ran out. I don't recall ever going shopping with any of my sisters and my mum was never in a fit state to go anywhere. Her husband used to beat her black and blue and even hospitalised her loads as well. My dad must have felt sorry for her because she was always at ours with her hubby on a Sunday having Sunday dinner.

I can remember my mum telling me how she'd tried throwing herself under a bus whilst pregnant with me, and that my dad hated me. I know I ended up running away from home and lived on the streets for a couple of nights. I think that's why. I was probably so confused. I was driven to getting pregnant by a man who was at least twenty years older than me. The night I told him I was pregnant, I was violently sick. I knew, I just knew I was, so he dumped me. My dad took it badly as well, he threw me out. I went to my doctor to tell him what happened, and he told me I would have to go to a hostel and more than likely have the baby taken off me. I was scared, I was really scared. Fate stepped in, though, as I was so ill, I was constantly sick, so dad let me back home.

If my mum bought anything for the baby she'd make my dad give her the money back. The way I saw it at the time, it would have meant less money for her beer otherwise. My sisters bought my pram and I was showered with baby items for her. A month before she was born, I ended up in hospital. As I was constantly being sick, my weight plummeted to 5 stone. I was put on drips immediately and still kept being sick. I even had a bad reaction to the iron they pumped into me. I managed to keep ice cubes down and that was basically it. I sailed through labour and she was born within four hours. She weighed 6lb 11oz.

When she was about three months old, I ended up being with her dad again. One night he'd asked me to have her adopted, as he wanted nothing to do with her, so I dumped him. A few days later I had the most horrendous miscarriage. At the time, I didn't know what was happening. I rushed to the doctor, he phoned an ambulance and told me what was happening. The nurses were horrid, they kept telling me what a stupid, naughty girl I'd been and that it was God punishing me. That incident was pushed as far back in my mind as it could go. I carried on for a few months. For some reason, I told myself I didn't deserve to be a mum and my daughter would be so much better off without me. I went to my friend's house with my daughter. I'd left her asleep in her pram. I went through cupboards looking for pills and found a near full bottle of sleeping tablets. I took them all and walked out of the house. I'd left a note for my friend and daughter. I can't remember what I'd written. I walked over to the golf course and hid waiting to die, but I didn't. I was found and rushed to hospital. I came to four days later to my dad and sister sitting beside me. That's the only memory of that incident.

I was offered a house in the same area and street I had lived in until I'd turned twelve, so I took it. I had no idea how to run a house. I barely had an income, let alone anything else. I had to wait months before I could move in as there was so much that needed doing to it. I bumped into a lad one night whom I ended up marrying. He liked my daughter and took us both out all the time. My dad got on well with him as well. We eventually moved into my house. My husband was eleven years older than me and it soon became apparent that he wasn't the same person if and when he was drinking. Yes, there were lots of fights because he felt he needed to control me all the time; whether it was because he was older, I don't know. We had another three kids over time and by the time I was twenty-three I had four kids.

Friends were a problem to him, he hated me having friends. He hated me going out (if I ever did, it was rare). I put up with his physical and mental abuse more out of shame because I'd seen the impact on my family of my mum and dad growing up. My kids weren't coming from a broken home, no matter what I had to endure. It was my bed, I'd made it, and that was that. As long as I hid it from the kids, it wouldn't matter.

My second daughter was just thirteen when she phoned me one morning and told me she was pregnant. That was a complete shock. My friends were so mad with me because I hadn't dragged her to the doctors to have a termination. That's not me and there was no way I would have put her through that, it was her choice. We supported her and helped her. My granddaughter was born in 2000 and what a beautiful, loving experience it was to see her being born. I've watched the births of most of my grandchildren over the years, we have been so blessed.

My granddaughter was a few months old when I'd gone out one night.

What happened is something that I still have the odd nightmare about. I was raped. I knew the person, as I'd worked with him. I blacked out, the only memory is him standing over me telling me to pull my pants up and get up off the floor. I wasn't brave enough to go to court. It's a memory I wish I could erase. I remember asking my doctor if he'd shoot me. He gave me antidepressants instead. Yes, they helped. I'm glad that I took them because it had taken me two years to actually go out of the house on my own. Obviously, my kids and husband helped as much as they could. I was extremely saddened by David's co-workers though. They thought he was mad staying with someone who'd been soiled and was now dirty. In fact, they said he was brave. My husband always drummed it into me that to have a good marriage you had to have sex every day. I hated it, though. It became a chore, kind of like boring ironing or housework, but I always gave in. He was still constantly accusing me of seeing someone no matter where I was or wasn't. I just used to shrug all the name-calling off, I'd got used to it like everything else.

However, I did the most unimaginable thing I could have ever have done. I know hundreds of women would probably want to scratch my eyes out. I had a one-night stand. I felt at the time a tremendous amount of relief, I really did. I didn't go home, I stayed away. My hubby phoned asking if we could talk. I agreed. I was expecting him to hit me or something, but he didn't, he assured me we would work through it and we wouldn't talk about it again. Things were going well, I suppose, until we became homeless. We ended up moving in with my daughter for a while. We moved a few times and finally settled in the house we're in now.

A couple of years ago, my hubby had a heart attack. It scared the whole family. I've got to admit that was the scariest time, driving down to the hospital in Leicester, as that's where he was working. He was on the mend and was home for a few weeks then went back to work. I'd started an online business. I became wrapped up in my own little bubble and watched the world go by until one night my son tried to take his own life. That was horrendous. He'd tied a wire round his neck and, believe me, that gives me nightmares, the state his face was in. The police arrived to check him as he'd phoned them earlier telling them what he was planning on doing. The girls took it hard. I watched him like a hawk for months, even gave my job up, it really freaked us out.

I thought things had settled down then a few months ago I saw a message flash up on my hubby's phone. What I saw knocked the wind completely out of me. After weeks of me arguing with him and walking out, he admitted he had been friends with a woman for a number of years and had fallen for her. He also told me he was leaving me and then told me he paid for oral sex with a young girl. I know it was karma, but I asked why I wasn't enough, why had things turned out the way they did? His reply was our marriage had been shit for years. I realised exactly what he meant and that was communication. We'd taken each other for granted over the years and become complacent with each other. We'd actually never done anything romantic or had a night out together, which I think is equally as important. We are working towards making our marriage happier and better. We've been together thirty-five years and yes, things have been horrendous at times, for which I think both of us are partly to blame. People often ask why I'm still married or why did Dave stay? I think it's the kids and the grandkids that keep us together; we certainly don't hate each other, we get on. I have my online business that keeps me going as well as my grandchildren and Dave has his job. I have a dream and a goal that gets me out of bed in the morning.

★ ★ ★

Lorraine is fifty-four and lives in Bolton. Lorraine is also a colour me beautiful consultant, who matches your make up to your skintone. You can find out more about Lorraine, check out her Instagram account @lorrainescolourguides

21. Charlie

I've had a colourful life, but when the opportunity to feature in this book came up I held back. Not because I don't have a story, but more because I struggle to pick a single one. So many losses and lessons to choose from. With a 3,000-word limit for a girl that talks a hell of a lot, this would be challenge. So, I've decided to share with you the one I feel might help the most people. Let's dive right in…

On 18th March, my nan passed away. God, I don't think I'll ever get used to saying that. My nan was one of those women who was full of gumption. She sometimes had a sharp tongue, but she would go above and beyond for those she loved. She was the type of woman that you kind of thought would be around forever.

On the night my nan passed, I blew out the candle I had lit for her earlier in the week and whispered, "Good night." It wouldn't be long now, I felt it in my core. So, I did the only thing I could do at that time. I slept. A little before midnight, I woke to the news that she had gone. But what followed that same night I did not see coming. Funny how I'm a psychic and this one slipped from my vision.

That very same night, my mother and sister disowned me. It wasn't pretty. There were a lot of nasty words said as I sat on the opposite end of the phone silently sobbing. I'm not going to lie, this sent me into a downward spiral for a little while.

When you choose someone to protect you and it turns out they don't want to even know you, it makes you question everything. You go backwards and forwards over situations and conversations. And, of course, being psychic, I asked myself, "Why didn't I see this coming?" I saw the drama in my mind's eye, but I suspected it was the general family disagreements. You know the ones that happen when everyone is grieving. But I didn't see this. Funny how the universe works like that sometimes.

As I sat in a heap on the floor, I hysterically screamed at Ashley, "We can't go to bed until we work out the lesson the universe is showing me!" (You see there is always a lesson.) He smiled that knowing smile and, as he's not a man of many words, he quietly waited. After a couple of hours, I had written down the whole evening's events so I wouldn't forget and I took myself to bed at 4am. Still none the wiser on what fucking lesson I had to learn. This night would now be referred to as "my disownment".

And so, the downward spiral began.

The thing they don't tell you about grief is, there's no blueprint for it. Each and every one of us do it our own way and in our own time. I knew my nan wouldn't be here by my birthday. I predicted it nine months beforehand. So yes, I was expecting it, yes, she'd already sent me signs she was with me within days of her passing over. But still the grief had to be released. I'd experienced grief before, I lost my first teenage love when I was at college and my dearest best friend shortly after I returned from honeymoon. But this time it wasn't just grief. This was grief stuck under a pile of rubble that I couldn't get to right now.

I felt like I was wrapped in layers of angry words and screaming down the phone from someone who should have loved me no matter what or who I was. That was going to be the most painful part. Death I've come to accept. I am a psychic medium, after all. But my 'disownment', well that's on a whole other level.

I always believed I had a strong mindset. Suicidal thoughts were not something I could ever emotionally understand when I heard or read about them. Yet here I was, curled up in bed, engulfed in an agony I can only describe as soul pain. I didn't want to get out of bed, I didn't want to move, I didn't want to process the recent events or words in my head for another minute. I wanted to stop the train and just get off. I'd had enough. Everything ached. Heart, body and soul. They say the mind is so powerful, but yet so easily manipulated. I was beginning to believe my mother's words. This went on for weeks.

Looking back on that time, I truly believe that if it weren't school holidays and if the kids weren't home, things could have ended a very different way. As awful as it sounds, my kids saved me. They curled up in bed for cuddles with their Kindles whilst I slept. We ate toast and crumpets for a lot of meals and they never once complained. Hero would put both hands on my tear-tracked cheeks and whisper, "I love you oceans, Mummy," when he thought I was asleep. And Boo Bear would sing me Easter songs and read to me about the fairies and the earth. I truly pray that they don't remember this time, or that if they do, they can see the process and the strength I eventually found. Now it wouldn't be fair to not mention my other half here because he did more than his fair share. He cooked, he cleaned, he bought me an essential oil diffusor and oils in the hopes of relieving my unbearable headaches. He encouraged me to leave the bedroom, to eat and to slowly begin to pick up the pieces.

I was also so very lucky to have my tribe around me. Although I may not have shown it at the time, their gentle words and the simple "Are you OK today?" text messages kept me in check with myself. I truly am lucky to be surrounded by wonderful people. The mind plays tricks on you; once that chimp is out and running free, that's when you need a team to get that monkey back in its cage. I will always be grateful for those people.

But the one text from a friend that truly saved me said simply this: "Google Narcissist". And I did just that. From the moment I clicked on the first website it became clear, all the years of ultimate highs and lowest of lows, the mind games and the constant need for attention. You cannot win when dealing with narcissistic behaviour. If you don't know what a narcissist is then stick your bookmark HERE and go Google it. This is your call to action. I guarantee you'll know at least one. Then when you come back, we can continue. Go on, these two minutes could change your life. Sounds dramatic, but honestly do it and come back.

So now we are on the same page, I'll continue.

The nights were the worst. My husband would hold me as the hot tears ran down my face and onto my pillow. Then when he had fallen into a deep sleep I would just lie there with my thoughts in the moonlight. It always seemed pointless going to bed as, however hard I tried, I didn't feel like I'd ever really slept. I'd recall all the mistakes I had made, all the daft things I had done when I was young. Every time I struggled with money or my kids. Every heartache and every loss. Well I couldn't fit it all into one chapter that's for sure. But you get the picture.

One night, I tossed and turned through my nightmares, you see they couldn't be dreams because I was replaying the same words over and over: "I'm alone, as I deserve to be. I'm the most selfish person to walk this earth". It went round and round on shuffle and repeat. Like a voiceover with clips of every mistake I'd made in the past twenty or so years. In the hopes of breaking the cycle, I got up and went downstairs and made a hot drink. The dog looked surprised to see me in the living room and happily curled up on my feet in the corner of the den. As I sipped my tea, my breathing began to slow, and my eyes got heavy. So, I put down my cup and let myself rest awhile.

The den is where I've always meditated in this house. It's the space I work from and the space every visitor is drawn to. Maybe it's the fresh white walls or the morning sunshine that shines through the window. Or the fact the energy in that room is almost like it's hugging you. So, it's no surprise that when I sleep in that room it's heavy and often my dreams are filled with messages from my spirit guides. This night in the den was no different. I saw my spirit guide Simba standing behind me as I was writing. But the thing that stood out to me most was I was in black and white and everything around me was in colour. The more I wrote, the more the colour slowly began to reappear in me, as if the writing was bringing me back to life. Then before I knew it, it was 6am and I was being climbed on by my bears asking for breakfast.

This was my sign.

You see some go to doctors, or see a counsellor, and this would be advised, but for me I wrote. I wrote firstly because I trust my guides, secondly because I was sick of talking about it and thirdly because it was my way of release. Little did I realise this would go on to heal me and help others.

I usually channel messages in writing, so for me this is often easier than speaking. I just let my fingers do the talking. From that point on I still wasn't ready to leave the house. Except for school runs, I curled up on the couch in the den and wrote; sometimes it made sense and other times it was just an A4 page of angry low vibe words. But I could feel myself getting lighter, not enough to want to venture out into the village for joy, but enough to have a shower and maybe even moisturise. Which was one step closer to being my old self again. Weeks passed and between Netflix binges of *The Crown* I wrote.

I wrote about the past, about days others would have forgotten and about my life up until now. I wrote about living in a mobile home with two children in the middle of winter with no central heating, I wrote about my dad leaving us when I was a child, how I felt about him having more children and the life they now live being the one I missed out on. I wrote about what it's like to see spirit from a child, I wrote about travelling 250 miles and moving into a house I'd only seen in pictures, in a village I had only been shown in a card reading. You name it, I've got it on paper. I collected pages like charms on a bracelet and it was beginning to fill up nicely.

One day, I sent one piece to my friend. I just felt I should and, before I could chicken out, I did it. Five Second Rule and all that. She sent this back: "Mate, it's beautiful, it's raw and it's honest. It's time to put yourself out there." I looked at the words and a wash of fear came over me. I'd done small posts on my Facebook page, they got a few likes and comments, but this was something else. This was me in all my... well, what's the opposite of glory? This was me in my emotional shit storm of a relationship with my mother. This was me sharing my raw thoughts with nothing held back. This was me admitting that sometimes the bad stuff happens to even me, and I'm one of the strong ones. I'm the one that supports other people.

Then that one niggle remained... if my birth mother didn't even like me, how was anyone else going to after they read my every thought? Would I lose clients? Would I lose friends? What would my kids think in years to come? Once it's online, they say it's there for good.

So, I started to read through my writing. Sometimes I would read it back to myself and the words just didn't seem like they had come from me. But they did. Perhaps they came from the girl I was at twenty-one, or the woman I was before I had kids, or the girl who came back from her honeymoon to find her best friend in an induced coma. Perhaps this was a new part of me I hadn't seen before. Wherever this girl came from, it was a part of me that I would have to get used to.

One morning, I woke up and I typed out a post straight to my Facebook wall. It contained the sentence: "Every life matters, every day has value". I found a picture on my camera roll from a few weeks before and I clicked 'post'. Then I carried on with my day. Nothing out of the ordinary, until lunchtime. I finished a card reading for a client and then checked my emails whilst shoving washing from the washer to the dryer… it's the mum in business way… one-handed housework is totally a thing, right? Like the bathroom being your second office… or maybe that's just me.

Right there, with one hand holding a wet Thomas the Tank Engine onesie, I opened an email that changed my life. It read something like this:

"Hi Charlie, I'm not one to comment on Facebook posts, but I'm going through a tough time at the moment and your words this morning have made me reconsider ending my life. I'm not out of the dark completely, but thank you for the reminder that 'every life matters', including my own."

I sat on the kitchen floor and I felt that woman's pain. Because I'd been there. I felt her struggles and how heavy she felt right now. And I knew she was meant to see my post that day. The universe laid it out before her to remind her that she mattered.

I cried. It wasn't a pretty cry or a movie type of single tear. This was ugly crying, face folding tears sitting on the kitchen floor with the dog sitting on my lap. You get the picture.

From that moment, everything changed. I realised you can't wait for someone to fly underneath you and save your life. Sometimes life may go a little dark and twisty, sometimes you get lost in the drama or in the worries of yourself and others. Could be for a week, maybe a month and sometimes you get so sucked in you don't even realise it until a few years down the line.

It was as if all in that moment I understood why I had to experience this excruciating amount of pain, from my father leaving to my mother's narcissistic behaviour. All the years of loss and struggle. The newspaper articles and family arrests when my granddad died. So much drama for one side of my life. I only had one question: when would it end?

I needed to see that I deserved more, no I deserved better. But also, I needed to learn that it's okay for people not to like me.

Now I had a reason to share my words, a reason to stop hiding behind branding without my name. I am my brand and that's not going to change, people are going to talk about me and that's not going to change. But what if they were talking about me for the right reasons? What if I helped people, what if I shouted from the rooftops "Be yourself no matter what!"

Within a week, I had begun to build a website from scratch with no previous knowledge. I'm more woo-woo than tech savvy, but within three weeks I was almost ready to launch.

I took every Facebook post I'd written and saved them as blogs right back to 2015. I wasn't changing my line of work, I was just embracing who I was in its full glory. This is how 'That Girl Charlie Edwards' was created. Here I am, this is me, flaws, mistakes and f-bombs in one big bundle.

It was time to embrace that I'm different AF, I'm hilarious, a little eccentric and full of magic. I'm kinda like Eleven from *Stranger Things* without the nose bleeds, ha ha! Some people aren't going to like me, some won't get it, but that's not my energy, it's all on them. And most importantly, I'm OK with that.

On the day of the website launch, I felt physically sick. I clicked the publish button and nothing happened, no one died, no one shouted, no one commented anything nasty. In fact, my client list more than doubled for readings because people connected with my blogs. They knew who they were working with and that my work is not only accurate, but it comes from a judgement-free space.

My brand and business have grown beyond my expectations on every level. I'm now not only booked weeks ahead for readings and healing, I'm being asked to speak at events about how the universe is always sending us signs for our highest good, how your story is your power and how you should never run from it. I am totally obsessed with women on the edge of change because I know your vibe and your story have a ripple effect on those around you. I've been at the bottom, now I'm not at the top, but I'm damn well closer than I was.

Which leaves me where I am today. If you finish this chapter and remember only one thing, let it be that: "Grit is the new Glamour".

Everyone has a story, and I mean everyone. Some are running scared from theirs, others hold it above their head like a crown. I choose to embrace mine like an old friend, knowing that it's a part of me. So, honour your story goddess, it's only one patch in your quilt, but no matter how dark or odd, it deserves to be included.

Oceans of Love Cx

★ ★ ★

Charlie lives in Yorkshire with her partner in crime and their two children, Boo Bear and Hero Bear.
Charlie is a transformational speaker and spiritual badass whose goal is to empower women and guide them on their journey. Whether this is through workshops, blogs, mentoring, readings or retreats, her vision is the same: to spread high vibes as far as possible and remind you that your inner Goddess already knows all the answers.
Her own book and oracle deck are due for release in autumn 2019.
You can find her anywhere under the name 'That Girl Charlie Edwards' and of course at www.thatgirlcharlieedwards.com

22. Joanne

Growing up, I felt I was from an ordinary and slightly boring family. We were run-of-the-mill, nothing remarkable; one brother, one cat, lived on a cul-de-sac. I did okay at school, never great, never rubbish, my hair was mousey, not brown, not blonde, my eyes were hazel, not brown, not green, everything was average, not interesting and not worth mentioning. Inside me there was always the feeling of not fitting in; I never felt like others, I always looked ahead to the next part of my life as the bit where I would finally feel part of something.

I went to an all girls' grammar school, which I 'did well to get into'. I was always in the middle set, always on the outside of the group, teased because of my frizzy hair, but never really bullied.

Nothing was really remarkable, but I never felt comfortable, relaxed, or able to be myself.

At the tender age of sixteen, I met my first boyfriend. He is now my husband of eighteen years and has been an incredibly supportive best friend since our very first date (where I forgot my glasses and made him turn back for them twenty minutes after setting off to the cinema! Some things haven't changed).

At seventeen, my parents separated, totally unexpectedly for my brother and I. One day my dad was there and all seemed 'average' and the next he was gone. It was a shock and things began to get a bit more tricky.

In sixth form, I entered the Young Enterprise Scheme and won the competition for the business to make the most money that year in our area, earning me an award for the best 'Managing Director' with a prize of an outward-bound weekend. I should have realised then that something had been stirred within me and would keep knocking for my attention for the next twenty years!

University was the norm, if you went to the girls' grammar school, and I never questioned if this was the right path for me. But first I had a year out, and taught English in a blind school in Krakow, Poland. I pitched up, without a coat and without any boots, to spend the winter in a freezing city, totally unprepared and having to grow up pretty damn fast.

My university course was chosen on my desire to help people and not being able to decide whether that should be in a medical profession or educational. Speech Therapy ticked both of these boxes and so it was. On my return, I studied Speech Science at Sheffield University, qualifying to be a Speech and Language Therapist in 1999.

For the next twenty years, I worked for the NHS as a speech and language therapist, but the entrepreneurial knock continued, and I always had a side 'project' going on from making and selling baby food to friends, running classes for preschool children to working as a private SLT outside of the NHS.

We had three children over the next six years and finally I felt I had found the thing I was meant to do. I love being a mum and I took the role very seriously, always making sure I was doing the best for them and reading books on parenting.

I still had a niggle, though, and this niggle continued to grow. I felt something wasn't right, but I couldn't put my finger on it. I had a motto that was 'If you can you should' and I lived by this, but was often left feeling exhausted, let down or taken advantage of, but never knew how to say no.

My relationship with my mum had never seemed like a 'problem' to me. I was always told I was lucky, and she was great, although I never felt good enough or worthy enough. I worried about her after my dad left and felt responsible, as though her happiness depended on me. The more I tried to oblige her, the more her expectations increased and there was always talk of 'if only I was this', and 'could I not be more like so and so'.

On the surface, I looked like I had it all, a big house, lovely children, a wonderful husband, friends, a great job, but slowly anxiety began to creep up on me. I felt I wasn't coping but had to hide it from the outside world.

Behind closed doors I was losing the plot and I couldn't work out why.

One night, seemingly no different from any other, I got off the phone to my mum and something clicked in my brain. I thought about the conversation and realised something wasn't right. I grabbed the iPad and Googled 'mum controlling me'. The next three hours I was lost in a web of information that suffocated and liberated me at the same time. It was as though my brain of thirty-five years was shaken up, and nothing seemed the same.

I began, over the next few weeks, to read advice and stories online about other people's experiences and they could have been written by me, everything was different to what it had seemed previously, the behaviours and conversations that had previously seemed 'normal' I could now see as manipulative and abusive.

I blamed myself for a long time, years in fact. I put into place boundaries that I had been lacking before and began for the first time in my life to say 'no' to my mum. My fear of her became very apparent and totally irrational and I realised this fear had been there since I was a little girl, and a lot of me 'trying to please her' was fear-based.

My mum reacted badly to my new boundaries. She must have been very confused, as I had never gone against her wishes. She punished me by giving me the silent treatment for two weeks. This is the two weeks that changed my life. During this two weeks, I began to make sense of it all and, with the space she provided me, began to realise I was more capable than she had told me I was, and my anxiety decreased.

This was the start of a long and treacherous road, a road that took me to very dark places, a road that had me question everything, know nothing and feel totally empty. Detangling yourself from someone who brought you up to only project themselves leaves you adrift at sea, in the dark, and not knowing what to do first. My fear response was huge too and I found myself in a permanent state of fight or flight, which made me ill. I couldn't show it, though, I had to keep my shit together and appear as the swan whilst all along I was gasping for air.

My husband didn't know what to do to help me, he didn't want to influence my decisions, wanted to support me, and had to soak up my emotions, as he was the one who bore the brunt.

Controlling people find it hard to break the control, and their efforts to get it back can be determined and forceful. Often, if they can't control the person directly, they control what others think about them and I found that other members of the family took sides.

But somehow I found it within me to stick firmly to my boundaries. We moved house to another area, staying for five months with my parents-in-law, who provided me with validation and nurture when I needed it most. We moved the children's school, straightened out our finances, and began a new life, bringing baby number four into the world.

My entrepreneurial spirit hadn't died and, just before my 'awakening', I had started and opened a preschool using my skills as a speech and language therapist to support the children's development.

I continued to portray a brave face, but not long after the birth of my fourth baby, I began to spiral down. Postnatal depression and anxiety came like a train and brought along with it panic attacks and agoraphobia.

So, I then found myself with a baby. A baby with a significant, undiagnosed tongue tie. A baby who was in pain and struggled with feeding, a baby who cried a lot, a business that needed me, postnatal depression and anxiety, a family who had disassociated itself with me because of how I had treated my mum and it was all just too much.

I was lucky to be taken on promptly by the local psychological services and be given the ideal person to help me. Little by little, I began to fathom it out, and work out what I needed to do, how to become a calm and rational person, to control my fight or flight, be less fearful and make sense of my life.

I began to enjoy making my own decisions and finding new interests. I was busy bringing up the children and made a decision to sell the preschool, which was a huge wrench as I had loved watching it grow and become a huge success, but it was the right thing to do for family life and for the preschool itself. It has continued to grow under the watchful eye of the new owner.

I vowed to be calm for a while, take stock and enjoy a slower life, but I couldn't keep my entrepreneurial spirit quiet for long and within a few months I had set up a Nanny Agency. It went from nought to ninety in a matter of weeks and I wasn't prepared for it, or for the time it demanded. I found the words 'just give me a minute, kids' were never far from my lips. We took our first holiday abroad nine months later and the space made me realise this wasn't for me; it had taught me so much and I was so grateful for it, but it needed a new owner, so I sold it on my return from holiday.

A 'friend' persuaded me to start the next business, holding weddings on my parents-in-law's farm. The next life lesson I needed was right there. It didn't go well from the start, this person really duped me and, worse still, then spread nasty rumours about me and my business within the industry. The feeling of being unheard and 'badly done to' rose again and, for the first time in my whole life, I became really, really angry; angry about everything, but angry mostly about always trying to do the right thing and others being able to sell a totally different picture of who you are. But do you know what, this anger was short-lived, and even more amazingly, it is as though I needed this experience to deal with the anger I had never released towards my family. I let it out and then it was gone. I didn't dwell, I searched for better ways to think, to forgive, to move on.

It was when I started to read more and look into self-development that things accelerated again, my confidence, self-esteem, happiness, love and gratitude went through the roof. I don't dwell on any of this stuff, I concentrate on the beauty all around and how lucky I am to have four amazing children and the best husband!

I always felt like my job in the NHS was not for me, I was a square peg in a round hole. Colleagues would tease me about my 'other entrepreneurial life' and would ask 'what are you up to now?' I always knew I wanted to be able to work on my businesses full-time around the children but was always fearful of money and not having a regular income.

It is when, during my self-development, I realised money was merely a mindset, and actually there was never going to be the perfect time to leave a regular income, that the decision came to finally say goodbye.

I had added a bell tent party business to my arsenal, with the intention of providing wedding creches with the nannies on the agency books. When I realised the agency was too much for me, I continued building up the tent business, putting party tents up in gardens and at weddings and then added indoor tent parties for the winter. I loved the opening it brought for my creativity and the smile it puts on people's faces. I then realised I could spread the love further afield and developed a franchise to sell, which is growing slowly and organically. Having a team is fantastic and I love the fact that my tents go up all over the country.

The tents have allowed me to leave my role in the NHS, and although I was so sad to leave my friends, I was excited to grow the tent business and work on setting up a new business aligned with my values and my passion.

For the first time, I took time to think carefully about what I wanted. I worked on my money mindset and got clear on my life goals. I committed to working with a coach who helped me to gain clarity and put into place a tried and tested strategy.

The outcome of several months of work is an online Speech and Language Therapy business enabling me to help parents of young children with developmental language difficulties. In the process, I have found my tribe, found people who lift me up and am enjoying life for everything it has to give.

I have learned so much over the last few years, it has come with such heartache and I would never have chosen this path for myself. We all know the old adage, 'If life gives you lemons, make lemonade' and, in a roundabout way, that is what I have done.

Through this journey my parenting has evolved too and some of the strategies that may have been acceptable in my childhood, and I used when my eldest were little, have gone, and love is given with no conditions in our house. I encourage my children to be themselves, accept themselves and to learn from situations. We don't need punishments, just understanding and problem solving. The children are thriving, and we are so proud that we have parented differently and given the children a different outlook on life.

The most important lesson I have learned along the way? Self love is the first and most important: when you show yourself love, acceptance and gratitude, it overflows, it can't help it and it lights up everyone around you too, effortlessly. This is pretty tough when you feel unworthy and unlovable, but it is possible. If you had told me that seven years ago, I wouldn't have understood what it meant, and certainly wouldn't have known how to apply it to myself.

I don't want to leave you thinking that I am a finished article, but what I do know is that I am looking forward to the onward journey. I can see the path ahead and it is filled with flowers.

I want to thank my husband for his unwavering support, and those who have been there for me, even when I wasn't there for myself, you know who you are!

I want to wish you luck on your own journey and I will leave you with this: 'Don't let the bastards get you down, find your own way, if knocked down, get back up and don't stop until you find your soul's calling'. x

★ ★ ★

Joanne Jones is married to her soulmate and has four children; they all live in a little village in Cheshire. You will find Joanne most days behind her computer supporting parents of children with speech, language and communication difficulties, to learn the skills they need and develop the mindset they require to be their child's best therapist. When not working, Jo loves walking her two dogs, meeting friends for coffee and seeking new adventures for the family. To find out more about the support Jo can offer you, visit www.joannejones.co.uk

23. Katie

I sat and gazed at the consultant in front of me, nodding my head in an apparent show of understanding. 'So, you can see,' she said as she pointed at my MRI, 'that there is considerable degradation of the myelin sheath here and here.' She pointed at the screen with her manicured fingernails. 'The creation of the plaques in your brain and spinal column are conclusive,' she continued.

I nodded some more and blinked rapidly at the MRI in front of me. There was my brain – in carefully computer-generated slices – laid out in front of me. I poked habitually at my numb left arm and tapped my not-properly-working left foot with my still-functioning right foot... just to double check that said foot was still there.

It was.

'Do you have any questions?' she asked me. I gazed at her coifed eighties hair and kind eyes. 'Miss Peers-Johnson? Do you have any questions?' she repeated.

'Yes. Just one,' I replied. 'When will I get better?'

I grew up in south London in the eighties. My parents were kind and loving, slightly too over-protective and often wrapped up in their own complex and busy lives.

My father was an osteopath who worked from his garden surgery. My clearest memories of him when I was a child are of him playing backgammon and smoking. I learnt to play backgammon long before I learnt to read, and to this day I am still a formidable opponent.

My mother ran her own business at a time when women were still very much meant to be housewives, something she never excelled at. She was driven, intense and determined. And supremely good at her job.

Then there was my beloved sister, Lucy. She's ten years older than me and almost every golden memory of my childhood – from the earliest to the happiest – involves my sister. There has never been a cooler, kinder and more awesome big sister. I am fully aware of how splendid she is and to this day she still holds me up, dusts me off and sends me back on my way with my head held high. She is my greatest inspiration for determination, courage and down-right-kick-assery.

My parents got divorced when I was twelve but, even though they must have felt great sadness at the events that had unfolded in the lead-up to their separation, they tried their best not to project it onto me. And, as always, my sister protected me.

My dad moved out of London and eventually remarried a wonderful, kind and hilarious woman who still makes me cackle with laughter.

My mum and I moved to a lovely flat on the river just by Battersea Bridge and our lives consisted of school, London life and shopping on the King's Road.

When I was sixteen, I woke up to the sound of my mother tapping on my bedroom window. 'Katie, Katie, let me in! Let me in! I can't see,' she shouted through the window. I was dragged out of a teenage slumber into a nightmare. I opened the front door to my mum, who was leaning against the door-frame.

'What's happening?' I asked.

'I don't know. I need to lie down,' she told me. My hands shook and sweated as I dialled that well-known-and-hopefully-never-needed-number.

The second we arrived in hospital she had a major epileptic seizure. I was swept out of the emergency room and into a "relatives' room" by a nurse who asked me, 'Is there anyone we can call?'

I must have replied, as she nodded and disappeared to make calls.

I was utterly alone.

My mother was rushed into theatre that night. Months of operations, chemotherapy, radiotherapy and power shakes filled all our lives.

She fought with her brain tumour for six months until it eventually took her on the 19th November 1997. Exactly one week before my seventeenth birthday.

The next few years of my life are a blur. I retreated into books – both reading and writing – and avoided the world as best as I possibly could. I left school to hide under my covers.

I had several mediocre jobs, but I wasn't good at following rules. All I really wanted to do was travel. 'KJ,' my dad said to me. 'Be aware that once you start travelling, you won't be able to stop.' He said this as he said goodbye to me in the airport on my way to Australia. I was twenty years old and determined to see something bigger than the boredom and grief I was living in.

My first time in Australia took me on a great adventure both emotionally, spiritually and physically. I healed, expanded and grew on that sunbaked soil. Whilst I was travelling – and when I got home – I worked, but I wanted so much more than they could ever offer me. It was never about money. It was about self-worth.

I made plans to go to India, Nepal, Canada, New Zealand, walk to Everest base camp, the Santiago de Compostela. I thought about nothing else – escape!

At some point in this time period I started to get an unsettling tingling feeling in my left arm. It would come and go seemingly randomly and the general consensus from the medical profession was that I had a trapped nerve.

This went on for several months until, without warning, the tingling appeared one morning in my left foot. A painful numbness a lot like when you have pins and needles, and the blood is flowing back into the area. You can't feel it, exactly, but it hurts at the same time. Over the course of the next few weeks, the painful numbness began to spread from my foot to my leg. Then my body and my left arm. Accompanying this was a debilitating exhaustion that had me sitting at the bottom of the stairs and crying wearily to myself as I didn't have the energy to climb them.

By this time, I couldn't entirely feel my left leg, half my body or my left arm. I had to call into work sick day after day. 'I'm not sure what's wrong with me,' I'd tell them. 'But I can't walk properly.'

I slept for twenty hours a day and used what little energy I had to wash and eat. Each action took every iota of strength, grit and determination.

23. Katie

My left leg, left arm and the left-hand side of my body was almost entirely desensitised. I could still walk, but barely, slowly and with focused determination. Every movement either hurt or exhausted me. I was twenty-three-years-old.

I lay in bed one morning and thought, 'This can't go on.' I couldn't do anything about my body, but I could do something about my spiralling mental condition. I decided to stop thinking about what my body couldn't do and started to ask it what it could do. My eyes fell on my abandoned guitar in the corner of the room that I'd never found the time to learn to play. I hobbled out of bed, tuned it up and started to learn.

I was truly terrible but the action of doing and learning something slowly began to draw me out of my funk. I was still a physical wreck but refocusing my mind onto something that I had control over empowered me more profoundly than a pep talk from God.

This was mine and I could do it! Slowly, yes. But I could do it!

I felt so blessed that my hands worked enough to play. And there was the added benefit of not getting sore finger tips since my fingers didn't feel pain in the normal way.

The doctor finally referred me to a neurologist, but the appointment wasn't for another six months, so there was nothing to do but wait.

I gradually regained partial feeling over the months I was waiting and managed to go back to work part-time after about four months in and out of bed.

When I finally got to the appointment with the neurologist, I had done a fair amount of research regarding my symptoms and potential outlook. I wasn't at all surprised when she said, 'You have MS – that's Multiple Sclerosis.' I went back to nodding sagely as she pointed at my MRI scan. 'Given your recovery from your initial symptoms we are fairly confident that it's Relapsing/Remitting MS for now. Although that may change…'

'I'm not recovered,' I stated plainly.

The doctor sighed and looked at my floppy, disobedient foot and said, 'It's very unlikely that you will progress further than this point and that we will see any considerable improvement from what you see now.'

I looked at what I saw now – a desensitised arm, a numb leg, a foot that dragged along the ground when I walked, shooting pains all over my body and crippling, endless exhaustion.

I thought to myself:

FUCK. THAT.

I also cried. I grieved for the body that I once knew and took for granted. I cried for the youth that I felt was stolen from me. And I cried for the life that I might have led.

I then straightened up and dug my toes into my future. Well, I dug my right toes in. My left toes weren't up to much. I embarked on a lifelong journey to health – one that I am still on – and a journey that will never end.

I was lucky, my MS was Relapsing/Remitting which meant I could – potentially – extend the remissions indefinitely. I realised quickly that negative stress and burning the candle at both ends would lead to a relapse. I learned to plan each day to the letter to make sure that I didn't overdo it, walk too far, work too hard or do too much. Gradually, the feeling in my leg and arm returned! I was still in pain and the fatigue was still desperately present, but I was returning to something near normal. I learnt to listen to my body deeply, intently and without hesitation.

The fatigue meant that returning to work full-time was impossible. I just didn't have the energy that I once had. There are only so many times that you can call an employer to tell them that you are too tired to go to work before they ask you to start looking for a new job.

I decided to create a life I wanted – no matter how disobedient my body was – and that was one of travel. I rented out the house I had bought, took my remaining savings and hit the road.

I spent many years traveling – Nepal, India, Sri Lanka, Australia, New Zealand, Singapore, Europe – and working. I did what I could, saw what I could and if I was going to be ill then I was damned well going to be ill in the warm and on a beach. I managed to keep the MS sufficiently at bay whilst I was travelling as there are no demands upon you, other than the ones you put upon yourself. I was still in pain and the numbness would come and go, but it was tolerable.

When I met my husband, Paul – five years after I was officially diagnosed – I had met plenty of men in the intervening years who would run a mile when they realised that I have MS. I had grown used to it and expected very little from the men I met. Pleasant to have around but can't trust them in a combat situation – like a pretty pair of shoes that you can't run in.

Romantically, I told Paul about my MS on our first date and, instead of making his excuses and silently slipping away, he said, 'What can we do to help you stay well?'

His presence and love couldn't have come at a better time as about three weeks after our first date my father passed away from cancer of the oesophagus. He had been fighting it for several months and, although the outlook for him had generally been considered to be a good one, he went into a sudden and unexpected decline.

For the third time in my life I went into deep, heart-crushing shock. My father's death brought up all the pain of losing my mother, and I went through a second grief for her as well as the new grief for my father.

Paul stood by me and loved me from the first moment. He suggested I move in with him to allow myself time to heal. We barely really knew each other but we knew we were perfect for each other, and that was enough.

When I finally lifted my head from the first shock of grief, I decided to do some exercise. I very slowly started going to the gym and swimming. I realised the stronger I got, the fitter I got, the harder it was for my body to take sudden control of my limbs. Being strong made me stronger, both physically, mentally and emotionally.

In about 2012, although the MS was stable, I was taking a large amount of medication to control the pain in my side, hands and leg. Hot burning sensations, like scalding water running down my legs, plagued me and the crippling fatigue was an ongoing issue. I was working part-time in an okay job but knew that I wanted more. I wanted something, but I didn't know what that was or how to make it happen. So, I focused on the things I DID know. And trusted that the rest would come into focus when the time was right.

Firstly, I wanted to have a family.

My two biggest issues were fatigue and pain. I didn't think I could do anything about the fatigue, but I figured I might be able to do something about the pain. I took medication that controlled it, but it was ill-advised to take it whilst pregnant. As soon as I stopped taking the medication, I was gripped by debilitating waves of pain that were more than I could bear. I couldn't envisage a life without painkillers.

I had experienced acupuncture briefly in Australia – and my sister had had it in the past – and I thought, 'What the heck, I might as well try it.'

I started going to acupuncture twice a month. My goal was to drop the pain medication for my pregnancy, so I could reasonably carry a child without risking my unborn baby's health.

With the help of my amazing acupuncturist I managed to entirely give up the pain medications. For the first time in seven years I was pain free and it was exhilarating. It didn't happen overnight, it took many months. But what were months compared to a lifetime? I decided that I could achieve anything with time, perseverance and focus.

'If I can get pain free, what else can I do?' I wondered.

I started to visualise myself in a state of perfect health and with that mental image I knew what I wanted to achieve.

Along with acupuncture, I made some calculated decisions designed to enhance my health to the next stage. I got fit, went to bed early and ate (reasonably) healthily. I started to prioritise my health and self-care as top of the list. Not somewhere way down in the List of Adulting. If one decision to prioritise acupuncture can get rid of my pain, what else can I do to fuel my further recovery? I was already so much further than the consultant said I would be all those years ago.

I had been made redundant from my job when I was pregnant so, after my daughter was born, I was a stay-at-home mummy. I never intended to go back to work when she was little as I couldn't imagine how I would create a functional work-life balance. I got very tired and needed a lot of rest.

Then one day I made a keepsake bear out of my daughter's baby grows that she had grown out of. I put the pictures onto Facebook to show my friends and several people asked, 'Can you make me one?'

In that moment, 'Memory Zoo' was born.

My hands shook uncontrollably the first time I cut up a customer's clothes to make them into a bear. And not because of the MS – this time it was fear. Fear of failure, fear of doing it wrong, fear of having a business, fear of getting sick again.

I stopped myself short and redirected my thoughts. I thought about how far I had come from those days in bed with no energy and no feeling and I realised that I could do anything.

I could definitely make a keepsake bear. I visualised the glorious bear I knew I was going to make and got the hell on with it.

During all this time I realised that I wanted to be BETTER STILL. I wondered what else I could do to further my healing. During 'Dry January' in 2016 I accidentally hit upon an answer – I realised that alcohol made me feel incredibly ill. I had never drunk much – maybe one G&T a week – and hadn't given any dedicated thought to its effects. It's just what everyone does. I'd unwittingly been poisoning myself.

My energy increased tenfold just from stopping that one G&T a week. Initially, I stopped napping every afternoon; then I didn't need to go to bed at 8pm; and as I healed further, I started to have more energy than I knew what to do with. I began to run to burn off the excess energy. And all the time visualising my healthy, perfect body doing all the things I was told I would never do.

I started to have personal mantras that immediately changed my perspective from negative thoughts to positive ones. If I didn't feel brave, I repeated over and over, 'I am brave,' until I reprogrammed my mind to believe it.

Add these all together and I felt like an unstoppable super-woman! It appeared miraculous but in truth the individual aspects were so easy and together they were powerful.

I began to wonder how many other things I was poisoning my body with that I had taken for granted, and so sugar and carbs were the next to go.

When I feel my MS stalking me, I take my foot off the gas and allow myself time to recuperate. I down tools and retreat.

Memory Zoo has grown a lot since I started it four years ago and I have massive plans. I have two skilled seamstresses that sew with me in their own homes. I aim to create a business that reflects my ethics and my attitudes. I created it so that it worked around my MS, as really I had no other choice. It ebbs and flows with the lows and highs of my health. I push when I can. Rest when I can't. For me, there is no other option. My biggest priority over everything else has always got to be my health and making sure that my legs don't stop working. As they say – without health you have nothing.

My MS has forced me to be selfish and excellent at self-care in a way that so many people fail to be. I have been forced to make a functioning work-life balance model and I am so grateful! We all have 'things' going on in our lives that interrupt our flow. By giving those things ownership, you can address them and move on with grace. If I feel down and out, I go for a run and visualise my perfect reality. I feel that image in my mind, smell it and absorb it. Then I know what I'm working towards. I need to remember just how insanely lucky I am to have legs that can run!

I might step from Relapsing/Remitting MS to Secondary Progressive. I might discover that I wake up one day and can't walk anymore. Or I might go blind.

This, for me, is an excellent thing. It allows me to constantly step out of my comfort zone today because tomorrow it might not be possible to do so. I constantly do things that scare me. Every time I release a new product and think, 'What if this bombs?' I stand up and shout: SO. FUCKING. WHAT? Have you still got legs?! YES! Then let it bomb! And you will dance on its stinking grave.

And sometimes things DO bomb and that's okay. I refuse to get to the end of my life – which I intend to be a long and healthy one – and say 'I wish I'd done that.'

And you can too. If you've ever been sick, down, grief-stricken, laden with fears or doubts, I urge you to develop a system for health that works for you. Visualise your perfect life and go for it! Throw caution to the wind! The very worst that can happen is that whatever it is doesn't work. You might lose face, patience or money but they are all things that can be regained.

What can never be regained is time. And what time is better to get well and do the things that drive you, fuel you and make you who you are than now?

23. Katie

★ ★ ★

Katie lives and works in Portishead, Bristol with her husband, daughter and very naughty dog. She loves walking the dog, exercising when her body allows it and creating beautiful things. She can often be found knitting, sewing, crocheting or writing her way through life. You can find her at www.memoryzoo.co.uk or through social media.

24. Emma B

Hi, I'm Emma, and I'm privileged to be able to share my story of love, life, betrayal, IVF, loss, babies and elephants with you all. My friends laugh at how many jobs or careers I have had. I call myself a 'Jill of all trades and Mistress of none' but I think life is for the living and it's important to grab opportunities whenever they arise. If we all waited for the perfect time or moment to try something new, we'd never do anything.

I grew up in Cheshire in the seventies with my mum and younger brother. When I was nine, along came my stepdad. My new baby brother, whom I adored, arrived when I was twelve.

But life in the 1970s and 80s was different, and things weren't discussed or dealt with as openly as they are now. So, when I was touched inappropriately by a man my mum worked for, she was advised by a lawyer friend to 'just let it go' as it would be difficult to prove and traumatic for me at the age of seven to go through the courts system; particularly as this man was a well-respected member of the community.

Fast forward to fourteen, and I was at a party with friends and a bit tipsy when a boy I thought was my boyfriend decided 'No' didn't mean 'No'. My friend took me to get the morning after pill the next day. I told no one.

I went to a Convent school run by nuns. I didn't feel like I quite fitted in. All the girls in my family had been there and let's just say, when I was caught truanting and drunk at fourteen, I didn't exactly make my family proud.

School finished and, at sixteen, I went to sixth form college, which didn't last long as I fell in with a bit of a party crowd and spent much of my time visiting the local friendly drug dealer's pub. How nothing horrible ever happened to me doing this, I'll never know, but thankfully I escaped from those adventures unscathed, if not well educated in the different varieties of marijuana. After being caught doing Poppers in the smokers' common room, yes there was such a thing in the eighties at college (smokers' common rooms were the place to be), I was politely asked to leave.

At eighteen, on my best friend Gary's birthday, we went to town to celebrate, and a college friend of his, a fellow musician, joined us; Jon. The first night we met, we hit it off instantly. We sat up talking the entire night after everyone else had fallen asleep. Jon walked me to the bus stop the next morning, and we shared a kiss. We fell madly in love and were inseparable.

When another friend pulled out of a holiday to Tenerife over New Year with Gary and his parents, Jon stepped in at the last minute. On the 2nd of January, the day they were due home, after phoning and being told Jon was asleep, I went to Gary's parents' house. Gary met me in the kitchen, and told me Jon was gone, he was dead. He had drowned in a freak accident on New Year's Eve afternoon. I don't remember much other than screaming and apparently punching the hell out of him as I howled, "No No No!" Suddenly hands were on me and held me as I collapsed sobbing, and I found I was in my mum's arms; she had been waiting for me to arrive. At nineteen, I didn't know how to process this, I was grieving. After about six months, I found my grief embarrassed and made people uncomfortable. So, I started to hide my feelings, and I hid them pretty well, but it always was and still is there; he'll never be forgotten, and twenty-five plus years later a song or odd flash of someone with beautiful dark, floppy hair can transport me right back to when we were together. And I wonder about what could have been.

I knew what I wanted to do and had done since I was nine years old. I was going to be an actress. I applied for various drama schools in London. I was successful and was offered a sought-after place, but Jon had died, and I didn't feel confident going away and starting my new life so far from home.

So, I moved into a shared house with some student friends and we had a ball. I started working at The Royal Exchange Theatre in Manchester and auditioned again the following year. This time I was offered a place at The Arden School of Theatre.

After my first year of training, I went travelling the western coast of Australia for three months living in a VW Combi, with no kitchen, toilet or shower, with my boyfriend. We had a fantastic time bathing in waterfalls and swimming with dolphins. Within a few days of us returning we were involved in a serious car accident when someone ran a red light and hit us. I had broken my back and was lucky not to be paralysed. I spent the following year recovering and was desperate to get back to college.

Although drama school was fun and I learnt lots, it ultimately led to a path of not much work and general unemployment.

I did meet my husband there. We were friends first, and romance blossomed; we got engaged and then married while travelling New Zealand after graduating in 1997.

I didn't do well sitting around and not 'doing' something with my life. After a few months of sitting around back in the UK, I started teaching English and Drama at college level and found I really enjoyed it. I think I'm naturally bossy, so teaching suited me. I taught there for three years.

Then I became restless, again I wanted to do something with animals, but not just any animals. Somehow, I blagged my way onto a graduate placement at Chester Zoo and worked with the orangutans, chimps and Madagascan lemurs there. I adored working with the animals, even if on my first day I attempted to clean out the sleeping quarters but wasn't too good with the jet hose and ended up covered head to toe in chimp poo and urine.

Working with primates further fuelled my desire to work in wildlife conservation in some capacity. I went on a three-month placement to a Game Reserve in South Africa. I LOVED every second of it and learnt so much about the wildlife, the stunning country and its vast beauty. I learnt how to shoot a gun, a necessity in those parts. I learnt how to inject a gemsbok (African antelope) in the back of a truck. I learnt how to be part of a game capture in the middle of the night and jump off a truck before it's actually stopped, and I learnt how to dress a heavily-sedated but still awake wild lion's injured paw under armed supervision. It was exciting stuff!

When I arrived home, I cried for weeks and felt claustrophobic being back in the UK. After a few weeks of feeling sorry for myself, I rang the local university to find out if there were any short courses in conservation or animal studies I could attend. Quite by chance, I was put through to a lecturer who invited me to come in for a chat. When I got there, I realised it was an interview for a Master's Degree in Conservation Biology. Somehow, with only a degree in Performing Arts to my name, I blagged my way onto the course. My thesis was on captive elephant behaviour, which I completed at Chester Zoo.

It was the hardest academic thing I have ever done in my life, and it nearly killed me. I still shudder at the thought of applied statistics, but I managed by the skin of my teeth to nail it, and graduated with an MSc in Conservation Biology.

Restless again, and always having had the dream to live overseas, my husband and I applied for residency in New Zealand. We left our jobs, sold our house, gave away most of our stuff and with just two huge backpacks headed off.

We went to volunteer at a wildlife and elephant sanctuary in Thailand for three months along the way. The Wildlife Foundation Thailand was a full-on place, run by a crazy Dutchman named Edwin, who is a famous conservationist, and a total lunatic to boot.

When we arrived Edwin pounced; he had read my CV, and the fact I had an MSc in Conservation Biology and had worked with captive animals previously, specifically elephants and primates, apparently made me perfect for the job as manager of the centre. I didn't have a clue, but again I blagged it and muddled through.

There were some crazy times, like when riding my rescued elephant 'Nom Phen' into the rainforest, she walked under an ant colony hanging from a tree and knocked down about 10,000 biting ants onto me. I screamed, desperately brushing them off me, still sitting on my elephant; it was like something from a horror film. The mahout jumped up and helped save me from the vicious bastards. The next day I still felt like ants were crawling all over me.

Plus, the time two of the volunteers accidentally let thirty-five monkeys out of their enclosure while feeding them and having to round them back up making monkey 'I love you' noises before they got lost or hurt and escaped into the rainforest.

When we were due to leave, Edwin asked us to stay and even offered to sign the elephants' sanctuary over to me as his real love was the primates' sanctuary adjacent to it, housing over 130 primates, twelve bears, a tiger, a crocodile and various other rescued wild creatures. I was thrilled!

Sadly, my husband had not taken to life in the wild and so to him the thought of living there was not high on his list of priorities. I had to decide between my marriage or my passion. I chose my marriage.

We arrived in New Zealand and fell in love with it instantly. I taught for a year before landing my dream job at Auckland Zoo as an educator. I stayed for three years and, by the time I left, I was the education manager and on the senior leadership team.

I then studied again, a Graduate Diploma in Environmental Management and was in the process of applying for my PhD when my husband suddenly agreed to go for IVF and try for a baby. I had wanted children for years, and it was a considerable emptiness I felt whenever women talked about their kids. My husband had previously been adamant he was not interested in becoming a parent in any way, shape or form, so when he changed his mind, I was overjoyed.

I went into IVF with blind confidence that, of course, it was going to work and work the first time. I became a dab hand at injecting myself in the stomach, not bad for someone that hated needles. Amazingly, it worked! I can still remember getting the call from the clinic sitting in my car in a car park; I was so excited to get the news, I cried tears of joy.

Nine months later and the centre of my universe, Theodore, was born. They did the usual birth checks, and all was well until he was about twenty-four hours old and one of the consultants thought they spotted something wrong with his heart. He was instantly whisked away to NICU for tests and monitoring. I could hardly breathe and demanded a wheelchair (I had lost a lot of blood and had collapsed after the birth, so wasn't allowed to walk anywhere).

I sat in NICU holding onto my baby's hand whilst he lay in the incubator, surrounded by some very sick babies, and I wept. Thankfully, all was well with his heart and after eleven anxious days we were allowed home.

Becoming a mother was the most amazing and transformational thing to ever happen to me. I had literally NO IDEA that I could ever feel like this and love this tiny human so much. He was and still is so breathtakingly beautiful to me that I would just hold him and look at him for hours on end.

When he was fourteen months old, I stopped breastfeeding so I could start the twice-daily hormone injections for the next round of IVF. I had decided that two years apart was the perfect age gap between my children. It had all gone so well the first time I was convinced it would be the same on this occasion. I was shattered when that wasn't the case. I went through a further eight rounds of IVF, trying all sorts to help; acupuncture, herbal teas and anything else I was recommended. Eventually, we decided to give it one more shot with overseas treatment at a wonderful clinic in South Africa.

Then a few weeks after paying for the clinic my life changed forever. I came home from rehearsals one night and my husband exploded. He launched into a tirade about how much he hated me and had done for years. He didn't love me, never had. I was fat, ugly, had let myself go and had ruined his life. I felt like I had been physically punched in the gut, I was winded. This was all a total shock to me. I had thought we were happy. I listened to his abuse in dismay for about an hour then I went to bed shell-shocked, knowing my marriage was over.

The next three months were a living hell, attempting to maintain a high-pressure job, commuting and caring for my two-year-old son, while enduring near-daily abusive phone calls.

However, I vowed instantly not to allow myself to become bitter or twisted, as that would only hurt my little boy and myself. I would find the positive somehow from this situation.

I was still determined to provide my son with a sibling. I intended to carry on with the IVF I had booked in South Africa. Only now I needed to arrange a sperm donor on top of it all. After various legal hoops I had to jump through, three months later my mum arrived from the UK, and we flew to Cape Town together.

We returned after an amazing sixteen-day trip and then had to wait ten days before I had the blood test. When the clinic rang to say I was pregnant, I couldn't believe it. Finally, I was going to have another baby.

Then at six weeks, I went to the bathroom one day, and there was blood. I was terrified and dashed to the clinic with my mum. We were taken into a room and told the doctor would come soon. I was shaking, the doctor came in and started the scan; I held my breath. "Everything's okay, I can hear the heartbeat," he said. I started sobbing.

So, I wasn't sure I heard him correctly when he said, "and I'm not sure how you'll feel about this, but down here I can hear another strong heartbeat. Emma, you're having twins!"

I remember the ferry journey home was quiet, neither of us spoke. Twins? Holy moly. Twins! Me! Really? After a day or two, I was thrilled, scared witless but overjoyed. TWO babies at once, how lucky was I?

An older mum having twins at forty-three and IVF babies, I ticked every box of high risk they had, and so had to visit the hospital every fortnight for scans and check-ups. I was told by the consultant how hard a pregnancy this would be and high risk. But I totally blew them out of the water and had a fabulous pregnancy. I loved being pregnant.

The birth went well in that both Saffron and Phoenix were born healthy and didn't need any oxygen or NICU time. Unfortunately, it didn't go as well for me, as I developed eclampsia and was very sick. I was in and out of consciousness for five days in the High Dependency Unit and don't remember much. But I bounced back to be told that it had been a close call, but all was well. The nurses had known I was strong-willed and a fighter as even in my semi-conscious state I had insisted they bring my babies to me and hold them to me to be breastfed (I was quite proud of that part).

Once I had my twins home, reality hit me like a ton of bricks. It was hard, very hard and I struggled for the first few weeks to find my equilibrium. I doubted my sanity. What had I done? On my own with a toddler, twins and no job? But thank God for my amazing mum. She had the babies sleep in with her when I was so tired I couldn't even stand up straight and would sit and listen to my fears and woes repeatedly.

The women in my community were incredible. Friends and people I hardly knew created a rota for meals and people popped in with healthy snacks and offered to hold the babies so I could rest. I will forever be thankful for my amazing friends.

Within a few weeks of the twins' birth I started performing comedy again, it was what kept me sane. A couple of hours a week when I was just me, not Mummy. I needed that small window of time out and fun, to help keep me sane.

Once my twins were here, I needed to figure out how I was going to provide for my three beautiful bubbas. I was and still am a wedding celebrant, but that is seasonal. I started copywriting and found that I loved it and people liked what I wrote. So, I created The Word Whisperer NZ, and within a few short months it took off. Thanks in part to my joining several women in business online groups, I discovered my niche, working primarily with women, as I could identify with them and their struggles. So, I changed my focus to working with female start-ups and small businesses. My company has grown so that I'm now booked up weeks in advance. I'm happy to say I haven't need to pay for any advertising, my business has thrived through recommendations and word of mouth. I enjoy working with clients all over the world.

Along with the comedy I perform, I wanted to write my own material, particularly about my children's antics. I would often be telling a friend a funny story about Theo or my twinadoes, and they'd say 'you should write that down' and so one day I did. That's how one of my other passions, my blog 'Don't Put Peas Up Your Nose' was born.

It's a blog looking at the funny and unexpected side to parenting written from my twins' perspective. I've had mums messaging me saying that reading about my crazy kids makes them feel better about their own little rascals or that they read my blog and had tears rolling down their faces at the stories. Such as the time I discovered my three-year-old daughter stuck hanging out of a bedroom window and had to call the fire brigade to set her free, whilst she happily giggled away and I nearly had a heart attack.

I have plans to write a series of children's books next year and earlier this year my first article was published in an online magazine. I was thrilled to be asked to write some further articles for them.

Like many mums, I need more hours in the day to make all this possible. But the biggest thing I can share is that even if I have doubts about whether something is achievable, I feel the fear and just do it anyway. We only get one chance at life, and I don't want to regret a missed opportunity. I want my children to see that anything is possible. That if you seize a chance, life won't be mediocre or pass you by. You won't get everything right, and it is OK to change your mind.

A positive mindset is what has kept me going even through setbacks, and there have been a few. My mantra is we only get one chance at life so grab it by the cojones and live life to the full! I try to and as a result I am the happiest I have ever been with my three rascals!

★ ★ ★

Emma is a happily flying solo mummy to Theo (seven) and twins Saffron and Phoenix (three). Originally from Cheshire in the UK she now lives on a beautiful island forty minutes' ferry ride from downtown Auckland. Emma likes to keep busy and as well as kid wrangling is a comedy performer on stage, a wedding celebrant, a copywriter, author and blogger. Sounds exhausting but it's just the way she likes it. Emma's mantra is 'Life is short so grab it by the cojones while you can!'

www.dontputpeasupyournose.com

25. Ellie

In my eyes, I had a wonderful childhood nurtured by two loving parents and surrounded by a large extended family. I am one of six children so the backdrop to our family life was always laughter and fun – at least that is how I remember it. I was encouraged to grow up with an independent nature with freedom to fully explore the outdoors. Our family was incredibly lucky to have a holiday house on a tiny island where we spent every holiday roaming free on remote beaches and cliff tops, scrambling over rocks and exploring caves. This ever-changing island landscape instilled in me from a very early age a deep passion for nature, which has continued on throughout my life.

As a teenager, I worked in many different jobs from cleaning, babysitting, fruit picking, legal secretary and pub cook. This led to an exciting opportunity to work on a Turkish dive boat, conjuring up Turkish food for thirty hungry divers in a sweltering and swaying galley. Everyone slept outside on deck and I would curl up on my mattress in the corner whilst the noise of holiday makers kept me awake until the early hours, knowing I would have to be up at five to start making breakfast! Looking back, it was a defining moment of my life. I learnt how to work hard in difficult and stressful conditions and realised just how much I loved scuba diving and boat life.

After studying Environmental Science at university, I spent a year travelling around Australia and married my wonderful husband Ian. We explored remote areas of the outback, met inspiring people and fell in love with Australia, making it our goal to move back there as soon as possible. Arriving back in the UK, I trained to become a Geography teacher and we built our lives around work and holidays, living on permanent countdown

201

from one adventure to the next. We decided to save money and live on a boat, teaching ourselves how to sail whilst spending the next five years arguing over who was Captain.

One of our holidays took us to Indonesia where we embarked on a boat trip to see the Komodo dragons. At one point we were cruising past a volcano, which last erupted in 1815 causing the largest and most catastrophic volcanic eruption in history. The hillsides, sand and sea were a very foreboding black colour from the volcanic ash and no villages had been seen for hours on end. Suddenly out of nowhere a boat of men came alongside us, waving at our Captain to slow down. When he refused they started firing machine guns across our bow. We were part of a small group of tourists in an extremely isolated and remote part of the world and not a single person knew where we were.

Fear and panic took over as our boat was forced to the shore and our Captain was manhandled off into the jungle. A group of men with guns stood on the beach staring silently at us for hours. My husband started preparing me for an emergency situation, strapping compasses to my wrists and knives to my ankles whilst I planned to jump over the side if needed. I was terrifyingly imagining the worst as only a few weeks previously, several tourists had disappeared and were thought to have been taken into slavery in a similar part of the world.

After an incredibly tense ten hours, our Captain was handed back to us at midnight, badly beaten, but we were allowed to go with a cheery, "Goodbye! Have a nice trip!" from our captors as if nothing had ever happened! It later emerged we had been stopped as part of a corrupt system whereby the boat owners hadn't paid enough money to sail past this stretch of land. We continued our holiday and left Indonesia with a great story and a renewed respect for different cultures and ways of life.

Back at home, life was going well, until a phone call came whilst I was teaching that shattered my world and changed my life forever. My mum had had a massive stroke on holiday in Cyprus and was in a deep coma. My family and I immediately flew out to be with her and the next ten days were spent agonising over every moment, holding tightly onto the smallest glimmer of hope. I remember singing her the Archers' theme tune and she opened her eyes and moved her leg. I asked her to move her leg if she could hear and understand me. She responded! I asked her more questions and she answered that she knew who I was and what had happened to her. I joked that this was extreme lengths for her to go to to stop me from moving to Australia and she opened her eyes and smiled. That was the last real memory I have of Mum, as she had a second stroke later that night and a few days later we made the difficult decision to turn off her life support, donating her organs to people in Cyprus. She was an incredible lady and she inspires me now to be the best mother I can be to my own children. I spent most of my teenage years trying to distance myself from her and yet now all I want to do is be more like her – something I will remind myself of when my own daughters are rebelling!

For the next three years, my life was grey as I struggled to adjust to this new version of me. I was twenty-six years old and had planned on Mum being around for my own children in the future. To suddenly have this rock and support taken away from me was utterly devastating and it was then I learned how pivotal a mother's role is. As soon as Mum died, my close family fragmented and split, each of us wrapped in our own grief and dealing with her loss in different ways, never to fully recover.

In 2008, our visas for Australia came through. After living on our boat in the UK for five years, we sold it and swore we would never live on another boat again. Years of gales, leaks, cramped spaces and no hot running water made us long for a proper house, yet within a month of moving to Sydney we had bought a bigger boat and were living on a mooring opposite the Harbour Bridge and Opera House. Behind us were multi-million dollar apartments and yet there we were paying a few hundred dollars a month for our incredible view, whilst hanging out our washing on the back deck for all to see! The warmth and friendliness of this boating lifestyle was very comforting, and I loved the community spirit and willingness to help. We decided even when our daughter was born that her first home would be the boat. She grew up there until eventually, at ten months old, I really and truly had had enough of boat life. We had no constant power, I had to wash all our clothes by hand, we had to carry all our water out to the mooring by dinghy and every time I went ashore I was plagued by fears of sharks looming up out of the depths to attack us! Time for a real house where we could raise our growing family.

Soon we had three children under five and we were looking for our next adventure. Ian's job meant we were flexible in where we lived, and I was very happy being a stay-at-home mum. We decided to move to an island in the Great Barrier Reef for a year before our eldest started school. After packing up our lives into two cars and two trailers and driving 4000km, a truly tropical paradise awaited us. Our new house had an amazing view stretching out over our swimming pool, banana plants and palm trees silhouetted by the setting sun. A year of bare feet, daily swims, alternative community, exotic animals and utter freedom from modern day society had us never wanting to leave and it was whilst on one of the island's beaches with my children that the next key pivotal moment in my life occurred.

A huge crowd of people had gathered to watch two turtles being released back into the ocean after spending a year in the Turtle Hospital. We formed two lines on the beach and the turtles were placed between us. As soon as they were released they raced to the sea and, within a matter of minutes, had disappeared. My four-year-old daughter started asking me lots of questions about the turtles, so we visited the Turtle Hospital where she discovered turtles are at risk from plastic in the ocean. Once my daughter made the connection between the plastic she saw on the beach and the turtles she had seen being released, she was on a mission to clean up the beaches. Together we would have to clean up the entire beach as with every piece she collected she felt like she was saving a turtle's life. It was seeing how literally she had taken this message on board that led me to start thinking about how I could share this story with as many children as possible and so the idea for my children's book was born.

I had written several books for children previously and sent them off to various publishers only for them to be rejected. Fed up with their lack of interest, I decided that I would do this book completely by myself and self-publish. Whilst on a trip back to the UK, I planned out the book during a long overnight drive and the next day, after only having half an hour's sleep, I wrote the story out in our caravan, drawing the first sketches using my children's crayons.

The first stumbling block was trying to find an illustrator. I had a very clear vision of the style of artwork I was looking for. My great-great-grandfather was a famous naturalist, writing and illustrating books about butterflies, birds and exotic animals in incredible scientific detail. It was his realistic style that I had in mind, yet I had no idea how to find someone who could replicate this for me.

It was during a chance discussion at my mother's group that I discovered my friend and fellow mum was an illustrator. As soon as she showed me her work I got goosebumps and I knew she was perfect. What later struck me about that moment was once our children are born we sometimes forget our own selves, as I had known this mum for many months, yet knew nothing about her life before she had children. Over the following months whilst we both juggled our children and pregnancies, the book illustrations slowly came to life as she managed to turn my crayon scribblings into beautiful artwork.

Ian and I now had four young children, including a newborn, a book that was almost ready to publish and we had just returned from a wonderful summer holiday. I had just dropped off my three-year-old son for his first day of preschool and was planning a relaxing morning with my new baby when Ian came running out. He had seen a Facebook message saying my younger brother Dom was missing whilst kayaking in Scotland. The next few days were a blur of extreme stress, anxiety and fear, as the RNLI, Coastguard and Police embarked on a five-day search and rescue mission to find Dom.

I helped coordinate a huge Facebook campaign and was doing live TV and radio interviews at two in the morning. I was poring over maps, contacting drone operators, kayak shops, psychics and keeping in touch with the police, hundreds of volunteers and community members, all of whom were risking their lives to find my brother – all whilst keeping up with the demands of a newborn with reflux. I was in the middle of a forty-degree heatwave whilst Scotland was enduring freezing gales and the rescue teams, my family, friends and local volunteers were scouring the clifftops in the pitch black desperately trying to find him.

I stayed at my computer for five solid days with barely any sleep. It felt like the years of chronic sleep deprivation with my four children had prepared me for this ordeal to find my brother. I was helping to coordinate the volunteers and keep people focused on positive thoughts of finding him alive. I was convinced that he could have made it to shore and was lying trapped at the base of the cliffs waiting for help and I held on to this belief right up until they found him.

I experienced a rollercoaster of emotions from despair to hope to utter desolation and profound grief as eventually his body was found, fifty miles away from the main search area. Through the power of Facebook, I was sitting in Australia at one in the morning talking on the phone to a lady who was standing on the cliffs at midday in Scotland looking at the helicopter and lifeboat as they retrieved my brother's body from the sea.

This was a tragic waste of life as Dom was a fit and experienced outdoor adventurer who regularly challenged himself on land and at sea. Unfortunately, that day he made a few poor decisions that ultimately led to him being caught out in the changeable winter weather conditions. He hadn't let anyone know he was going out or when to expect him back, he had his phone stored in the back hatch of the kayak rather than on his person, he went out by himself and he didn't have the level of experience for the changeable conditions. He also didn't carry a Personal Locator Beacon (PLB). This is a small, relatively inexpensive, wearable device which, when activated, sends a powerful signal straight to the emergency services via satellite, who can then pinpoint your location to within a few metres. And they work on land or sea. The rescue teams are directed straight to you without wasting any valuable time or effort in searching, therefore reducing their overall risk dramatically. Had Dom been carrying one of these with him on his trip then the outcome could have been very different. I felt very strongly that I didn't want any other family to suffer as we had done, and I decided to set up a charity called Plan B to raise awareness of PLBs and promote safety in outdoor sports in general. I have since made films with the RNLI and was extremely honoured to be invited by them to Buckingham Palace recently as a thank you for being involved with this effort – a truly bittersweet yet exciting experience.

I helped my family to plan a beautiful, natural funeral, even though I was still in Australia. I also had to plan a trip back to the UK with four young children. The thought of travelling all that way with a new baby, the disruption to the children's routines, the sheer costs involved, and the effort of packing was overwhelming. I hadn't slept more than an hour a day in the last two weeks and the absolute last thing I wanted was to take my children to my brother's funeral.

Following my brother's hearse to the burial site, over the hills in glorious sunshine was a key moment for us as we saw the beauty of the land we instinctively called home – it felt like Dom was showing us everything he loved about nature. Even though we had a well-established life, friends, schools and home in Australia that we loved, at a time such as this, it made us appreciate our family even more. Six weeks later we had enrolled the children in schools in Cornwall and Ian had returned to Australia to pack up our lives, leaving me with four children, four suitcases and a rented house to furnish.

Our children were growing and becoming more independent, which meant we could shift our focus to work. My brother kindly left me some money in his will, which meant we could finish putting the first book together. Dom had helped edit the book two weeks before he died, so some of the words are his, and we joked about him being a turtle ambassador, travelling the world sharing the message of the book. Having the same upbringing as me, he was also passionate about the environment and I am immensely proud that I have used his legacy to make a difference.

Self-publishing a book was a steep learning curve and the first version of the book was awful. Eagerly I awaited the print samples, only to be faced with a disaster. Pages fell out, sentences were cut short and the quality of the titles and fonts was shockingly amateurish. Lessons learned, a new front cover and a new printer and finally I had a book I could share and be proud of. The old adage "You get what you pay for" was very true for me and finding the right people to work with, even though it cost more than I originally budgeted, was the best decision I made for the business in the early days.

Those first few orders were so important in gaining confidence and knowledge. As soon as I was confident in the book, I put all my passion and enthusiasm behind it and what a difference that makes! Initially when speaking to stockists, I had to bluff my way through as I had no knowledge of how the publishing industry works, what wholesale prices I should be offering or even what terms I should operate on. I sent copies of the books off to everyone I could think of and most were supportive in some way, from small, local bookshops to large national marine charities, right the way up to the legendary Sir David Attenborough. To receive a personal letter of congratulations from the most prominent global advocate for our environment was an incredible feeling and added credibility to my discussions with potential stockists. I quickly gained recognition in the press, appearing on BBC Radio and TV and also in *The Guardian*, *Metro*, *Huffington Post* and *Mail on Sunday*.

With each successive print run, we could increase our order size and so reduce costs and I now have 10,000 books dotted around my house. My belief in what I was doing grew daily and I managed to write and publish my second true environmental children's book just three months after publishing the first. I also embarked on a book tour around Cornwall visiting forty different schools in five months, reading the books for free in assemblies and workshops to over 10,000 children. During conversations with teachers, children and parents I discovered that these books were so much more than just picture books. They were the inspiration a whole community needed to change attitudes.

As the *Blue Planet* effect took hold, I realised my books were very well placed to deliver this message into schools. I put together teaching resources and, with feedback and support from many prominent people in the ocean plastic movement, my idea for getting the books into every primary school in the UK began to develop. I contacted communities and volunteers around the country asking for their support to get the books into every school in their towns and cities through local business sponsorship. By targeting all the schools at once you effectively teach a whole generation about the problem. Children are inspiring their teachers, parents, schools and wider communities to take action. They are organising beach cleans, litter picks, setting up recycling stations and importantly using their persuasive writing to write letters to local businesses asking them to stop their use of single-use plastic. Between all those children they probably have links to every single business in the community, so it becomes an easy decision for a local business owner to make.

So far, the books have reached almost 500,000 children around the world and I am setting up Crowdfunder campaigns to get the books into every primary school in the UK, region by region. My third book about a whale is due out this month and I also have plans for sponsored litter picks in schools in the UK to fund the translated books overseas, reaching millions of children in schools in countries such as Indonesia, The Philippines, India and Kenya. By sharing this message with children, we are teaching them from an early age to care for our environment and instilling in them habits that will become second nature.

Currently, the business is run from a caravan in the garden of our rented three-bedroom home, which is crammed full of boxes of books. There is no extravagant lifestyle or money to spare as every single penny goes back into the books. We juggle the balance of family life and working from home by taking it in turns to parent but make sure we have one day at the weekend where we are all together as a family as well as making the most of school holidays away in our caravan.

The knowledge that I am just a normal, chaotic, stressed mum who happens to have been in the right place at the right time to bring these books to life and share this message with millions of children makes me smile as I realise there is no magic formula; it just comes down to hard work, tears and a lot of luck. I feel my brother strongly beside me through this journey as he both drives me on and laughs at my mistakes and he always did want to be part of something big. Well here is his chance and I hope I make him proud every day to see the books he has been so much a part of, changing the world, one piece of rubbish at a time!

★ ★ ★

Ellie Jackson is a children's author, environmental campaigner and mum of four young children. She writes books about global environmental issues for primary and preschool-aged children and aims to get her three books on ocean plastic into every primary school in the UK.

To find out about the books into schools project, teaching resources, to become a stockist or to order signed copies of the books please visit www.wildtribeheroes.com

Printed in Great Britain
by Amazon